The Art of
South
Indian
Cooking

The Art of
South
Indian
Cooking

Aroona Reejhsinghani

JAICO PUBLISHING HOUSE

Mumbai • Delhi • Bangalore • Kolkata
Hyderabad • Chennai • Ahmedabad • Bhopal

Published by Jaico Publishing House
121 Mahatma Gandhi Road
Mumbai - 400 001
jaicopub@vsnl.com
www.jaicobooks.com

THE ART OF SOUTH INDIAN COOKING
ISBN 81-7224-057-0

First Jaico Impression: 1973
Fifteenth Jaico Impression: 2006

Printed by
Snehesh Printers
320-A, Shah & Nahar Ind. Est. A-1
Lower Parel, Mumbai - 400 013.

CONTENTS

Pages

Pages

Rice Dishes

Sweets And Desserts

INTRODUCTION

South India is a rich and a fertile region. It has mountain scenes of great beauty, great water-ways with peaceful lagoons and palm-fringed shores. South India besides having great visual beauty is also famous throughout India as the region of temple-towns, for nowhere in India are there as many temples of exquisite beauty as in South India. It is also famous for its dances Bharatnatyam and Kathakali which are pure forms of classical dances which have been in vogue for several centuries and unspoilt by passage of time and lastly it is famous for its distinctive and unique cuisine.

Who in India has not heard of idli sambhar, dosa, avial and uppama? Besides these dishes which have acquired national fame there are the world famous madrasi curries which are very hot and spicy and very delicious. South Indians like their food hot and a true South Indian can eat a number of chillies at a time without batting an eyelid. Besides chillies they are also very fond of rice and dals. At every meal they want rice in one form or the other, therefore one finds rice as the base of almost all their eatables from snacks right upto sweets and desserts. Dal is a natural accompaniment to every meal, it is also used for seasoning almost all types of dishes.

South Indian food is unique, colourful and satisfying. If you try it just once, you will want to try it over and over again because in spite of being very hot and spicy, it is a delight of every gourmet's heart. South Indians from Tamil Nadu and other places use sesame seed oil for cooking their food, whereas Keralites make use of coconut oil, but you can substitute any oil for them and you will get equally good results. I am grateful to Mrs. Saraswati Srinivasan and Mrs. Lalitha Bekal for lending me some of their recipes to include in this book. All the recipes in this book are tried, tested and authentic, and exclusively from South India. I hope you will love preparing these recipes as much as I have loved writing them down for you.

AROONA REEJHSINGHANI

GLOSSARY

English	Hindi	Tamil

Vegetables:

English	Hindi	Tamil
Ashgourd	Petha	Paringi
Brinjal	Baigan	Katrikai
Bittergourd	Karela	Pavakkai
Banana flower	Kele ka phool	Vazhaipu
Banana stem	Kele ki dandi	Vadetunde
Banana (raw)	Kachakela	Varikai
Cucumber	Kakadi	Velerikai
Chillies (green)	Hari mirchi	Moloogah
Cluster beans	Gavar	Koturkai
Carrots	Gajar	Manjal Mullangi
Cabbage	Hund or patta gobi	Mutacose
Cauliflower	Phool gobi	Pukkirai
Drumstick	Shingh fali	Mooroongakai
Mango (raw)	Kacha amb	Mangai
Neem flowers	Neem ke phool	Vepabu
Ladies fingers	Bhendi	Bandakai
Lime (sour)	Limbu	Yellumshikai
Onions	Pyaj	Vungium
Pumpkin	Doodhi	Poosanikai
Potatoes	Alu	Urulaikhizangu
Peas (green)	Mutter or watana	Patani
Radish	Muli	Mulangi
Sweet potatoes	Shakurkandi	Chakrevali
Tomatoes	Tamatar	Thuckaley
Yam	Suran	Senaikizhangu

Herbs

English	Hindi	Tamil
Corriander leaves	Kotmir	Kothamilee
Curry leaves	Curry patta	Karuvepillai
Mint leaves	Phodina	Pothine
Fenugreek leaves	Methi bhajee	Mendiumkerai

Fruits & Nuts

English	Hindi	Tamil
Almonds	Badam	Vathumai
Apple	Sev	Appilparam
Banana	Kela	Varaiparam
Coconut	Narial	Tengenikai
Coconut (dry)	Kopra	Koprai

English	Hindi	Tamil
Cashewnuts	Kaju	Mindri
Groundnuts	Moongfali	Kadlekai
Jackfruit		Palepadam
Papaya	Papita	Papali
Pineapple	Ananas	Anasi
Mangoe	Aamb	Mambaram
Pistachio nuts	Pista	Pistach kottai
Raisins	Kishmish	Munthiri

Spices

English	Hindi	Tamil
Asafoetida	Hing	Perunkayam
Cardamoms	Elachi	Elam
Corriander powder	Pissa hua sukha dhania	Kotumalipudi
Cloves	Lavang	Lavangum
Corriander seeds	Sukha dhania	Kotumalivarai
Cinnamon	Dalchini	Karuvapadai
Chilli powder	Pissi huai lal mirchi	Moolgapudi
Cumin seeds	Jeera	Jeerugum
Caraway seeds	Kala jeera	Kalijeerugum
Ginger	Adhruk	Injee
Dry ginger	Saunt	Chuchoo
Garlic	Lasun	Mallaypoondu
Fenugreek seeds	Methi	Mendium
Mustard seeds	Rai	Kadugu
Mace	Javitri	Japatri
Nutmeg	Jaiphal	Jathikai
Peppercorns	Kali mirchi	Milagu
Poppy seeds	Khuskhus	Kasakasa
Turmeric powder	Huldi	Munjal
Saffron	Kesar	Kungumuppu
Sugar	Shakur	Chuckeray
Salt	Namak	Hoopoo
Sesame seeds	Til	Yellu
Jaggery	Gur	Vellum
Tamarind	Imli	Puli

English	Hindi	Tamil
Pulses & Lentils		
Green grams	Masur dal	Paitum purpoo
Bengal grams	Channa dal	Cuddalay purpoo
Toor grams	Toovar dal	Toorai purpoo
Black grams	Urad dal	Ooloonthoo pur-poo
Red grams	Masur	Masur purpoo
Flours		
Flour	Gheun ka atta	Goddumue
Refined flour	Maida	Maida
Gram flour	Besan	Kudlamae
Semolina	Suji	Ravai
Sago	Sabudana	Javorsi
Vermecelli	Seviyan	Semiyan

HELPFUL HINTS

If you keep aside peeled and sliced potatoes, sweet potatoes, brinjals and raw bananas they catch an unattractive brown colour. To prevent this discolouration always keep them immersed in plenty of water to which a little salt has been added. In order to prevent the pungent odour of onions from bringing tears to your eyes, always cut them immersed in water. Water helps in absorbing their pungent odour.

Put a piece of bread wrapped in a piece of muslin cloth in the water in which you want to boil any strong smelling vegetables like cauliflower, cabbage etc. Bread will help in decreasing their strong odour.

To remove bitterness from fenugreek leaves, sprinkle the leaves with salt and set aside for 15 minutes or so, then squeeze out all the water, wash the leaves thoroughly before putting them to cook.

To remove smell from fish, make a batter of a little gram flour, water and little turmeric powder and apply nicely on the fish. Set aside for half an hour, then wash nicely and use it in any called for recipe.

To get strong aroma from saffron always soak it in either hot water or milk for 10 minutes.

To extract thin and thick coconut milk nicely from coconut. Take 1 whole fresh coconut, grate it, then grind it finely. Now pour in it 1 cup water and place over a slow fire and bring it to a boil. Remove from fire, cool thoroughly then squeeze the liquid and the pulp through a muslin cloth until the pulp turns dry. For the second extraction of milk put in any amount of water as is required by you on the squeezed pulp, but it should not exceed 3 cups. Bring to a boil, cool and squeeze out the thin milk through a muslin cloth.

In boiling all kinds of dals, rice and vegetables skimming is most important. As the white frothy scum rises it should be taken off with the help of a spoon as both flavour and appearance of the food are injured by it.

Before preparing cauliflower put it in water to which little vinegar has been added. Set aside for 15 minutes and it will be free of all the dirt and insects.

COOKING GLOSSARY

Beat......to beat with a rotary beater, fork or a spoon any liquid or semi-liquid food with the express purpose of mixing that particular item of food thoroughly and making it smooth and free of any lumps.

Blend......to combine several ingredients together till smooth.

Boil......to heat a liquid until bubbles appear on the surface and vapour starts rising.

Blanch or peel......Cover nuts or tomatoes or whatever thing you want to blanch with cold water and bring to a boil, reduce heat and simmer gently till you find the skin of the thing you are blanching wrinkling. Remove from heat atonce, drain and cover with cold water then peel off the skin.

Batter......is a mixture of flour and liquid. The consistancy of batter is such that it can be stirred with a spoon and is thin enough to pour or drop from the spoon.

Chill......to cool food by placing it either in the fridge or on the ice.

Chop......to cut food into small pieces.

Combine......to mix two or more ingredients together.

Dice......to cut food into small pieces.

Dissolve......to melt.

Drain......to free a food completely from liquid.

Deep......to fry in plenty of ghee or oil.

Dough......a mixture of flour and liquid usually with other ingredients added. A dough is thick enough to knead or roll, but is too stiff to stir or pour.

Fry......to cook food in ghee or oil till it turns brown.

Garnish......to decorate food.

Garlic flake......an individual piece in a pod of garlic. For example the various flakes of garlic make a pod of garlic.

Grate......to rub food into small pieces on a grater.

Grind......to reduce food to a paste.

Gravy......liquid in which the food is cooked.

Knead......to work dough with hands pressing, stretching, folding and punching till it turns smooth.

Melt......to heat until the ingredients are changed from solid to liquid.

Mince......to chop food as finely as possible.

Pare or peel......to remove the outside skin or peel of vegetables or fruits.

Roll......to place a small ball of dough on a flat wooden board and roll it out into any shape you like with the help of a rolling pin.

Sift......to separate coarse pieces from flour, sugar excetra by shaking through a sieve.

Seasonings or spices......aromatic dried herbs and spices used to increase the taste and appearance of food.

Shred......to cut food into small long and narrow stripes.

Squeeze......to drain out the liquid from food by crushing or pressing between your hands.

Simmer......to cook food just below the boiling point.

Soak......to cover food with liquid.

Shallow fry......to fry food in a little boiling ghee or oil till brown.

Steam......to steam food is to cook food by means of steam generated by boiling water. The food does not come in contact with water. To steam food, take a very large dekchi or a vessel and fill it half full with water. Fit a steel or aluminium perforated rack or a colander in the vessel half an inch above the water line. Place the vessel on the fire and bring the water to a rolling boil. Place the food to be steamed on the rack and cover the vessel with a tight-fitting lid and steam for any length of time as advised in the recipe. Add more water if the water in the vessel is used up. For steaming kheema, pudding or other minced ingredients, first place them in a container before placing them on the rack. This is a much better method then boiling because in this method all the important nutrients are retained in the food.

PRESERVING FOOD

In these days of rising prices and food shortage the emphasis should be on economy. The first step towards economy is to prevent food from going waste by storing it properly. Here are a few useful hints which will tell you how to store different types of food-stuffs.

Put cream and cottage cheese in a closed container and place the container near the freezing compartment because they are highly perishable food items.

Hard cheese should be placed in a container with a tight-fitting lid. Put a big pinch of sugar with it to prevent the cheese from drying and place in the fridge. Outside a fridge you can prevent cheese from moulding by wrapping it in a piece of muslin cloth wrung out in vinegar. As the cloth dries, moisten it again.

Butter should be stored in a airtight container and then it should be placed in the coldest part of the fridge. Exclusion of air will protect it from reacting wiht oxygen to produce a rancid odour and flavour. Exposure to warmth and light hastens the development of rancidity and so butter should not be kept for long at room temperature.

All kinds of vegetables and fruits should be put in either plastic or paper bags and then they should be placed in the fridge. This helps in reducing the evaporation of moisture. If they are stored uncovered the crispness and flavour of both vegetables and fruits will deteriorate rapidly as water will evaporate form the vegetable and fruit tissues. Outside a fridge preserve them by putting them in polythene bags in which holes have been punched all over about 1-inch apart. When the bags are full, tie top tightly with a rubber band or a piece of wire.

Onions should be placed in plastic bags and stored in the vegetable bin. Onions will then not cause you to shed tears when you are peeling them. Outside a fridge onions should be stored in a loosely woven bag with good circulation of air. High temperature and humidity causes sprouting and decay of dry onions.

Potatoes keep best in a cool, dark and a dry place with good circulation of air. Light causes greening. If the potatoes are stored in the fridge, some of the starch is turned into sugar, giving them an undesirable sweetness. Potatoes which have turned sweet because of storing them in the fridge, will improve in flavour if kept at room temperature for about a week or so.

Refrigerate eggs in a closed container because shells of eggs being very porous allow access to moisture, bacteria and mould if left uncovered for any period of time. Outside a fridge keep eggs fresh by rubbing them either with butter or oil.

Wrap meat in wax paper and store in the ice box. Once you thaw meat never refreeze it again as it will turn hard after cooking. Therefore always thaw as much meat as is needed at a time. Outside a fridge preserve meat by sprinkling on it powdered charcoal. Charcoal is not only a very good preserver and purifier but at the same time it can be wiped off easily with the help of a damp cloth.

Place fish in a cardboard box and then pour in enough water to cover it. Put the lid on and then place the box in the ice-box. This way the fish will keep fresh for about a week. Outside a fridge preserve fish and all types of poultry by washing them in a lukewarm solution of $1\frac{1}{2}$ tsps. of salicylic acid and 2 cups water.

A simple domestic method to prevent milk from turning bad in hot weather is to wrap muslin cloth around the bottles and stand in a basin of water with the neck just protruding out of the water. Place the basin in a cool, dark and dry place away from light

You can prevent drinks and sherbets from turning mouldy in warm weather by placing the bottles in a basin of water with the necks just protruding out of water. Put in the basin a handful each of washing soda and salt. This is also a good cooling mixture. If you do not possess fridge you can cool anything by standing it in the basin of the cooling mixture for half an hour, but before placing anything in the basin place the thing in a closed container.

To prevent insects from attacking any dals, clean and rub on them a little oil and store them in airtight containers.

To prevent vermicelli and semolina from getting stale and insect infected, fry them in a little oil or ghee to a light golden colour and store them in airtight containers. Place the containers in the fridge or a cool dry place.

For preserving wheat for a long period of time, place in its container a handful of coarse salt and neem leaves. If your wheat is already swarming with insects do not throw it away. You can make it fit for consumption by washing it in plenty of water and then spreading it over a cloth and drying it in the hot sun for a day.

To preserve rice, rub it lightly with ghee or oil and then put it in a few flakes of garlic.

Safe-guard your ghee against rancidity by storing it in a closed container which excludes all air and light and place the container either in the fridge or a cool, dark and dry place.

PAPADAMS AND WAFERS

Cabbage Wafers

1 kilo cabbage, finely shredded. ¼ kilo urad dal. 1 tblsp. cumin seeds. 2-inch piece ginger. 6 green chillies. 1 tsp. turmeric powder. Salt to suit the taste.

Grind ginger and chillies to a paste. Soak dal whole night in water. Next morning, drain out the water and grind to a thick paste. Mix in all the above ingredients then take a plastic sheet and drop the mixture on it with the help of a teaspoon 2-inches apart from one another. Spread the mixture in a thin round shape. Cover the whole with with a thin muslin cloth to prevent mud and other insects from settling on the wafers and place in the hot sun. Dry for about 3 to 4 days, then remove the wafers carefully from the sheet and turn them over and once again place them in the sun to dry. When they dry completely, store them in airtight containers. When wanted for use, heat enough oil for deep frying to smoking reduce heat and fry the wafers quickly to a light golden colour. Drain them nicely before serving.

Petha wafers

250 grams urad dal. 1 kilo petha. 25 grams each of ginger and green chillies. 1 tblsp. cumin seeds. 1 tsp turmeric powder. Salt to taste.

Peel and grate the petha finely. Squeeze out all the water with your hands and set aside. Soak dal whole night in water. Next morning, drain out the water and grind to a thick paste along with ginger and chillies. Mix in the rest of the above ingredients and make wafers as shown in the above recipe. They should be fried in the same way as cabbage wafers.

Sago wafers

2 cups sago, 25 grams green chillies, ground. Handful of sliced mint leaves. 1 tblsp. each of cumin and sesame

seeds. 1 big tomato, peeled, depiped and pureed. 1 tblsp. beaten curds. Salt to suit the taste.

Heat 8 cups of water to boiling, put in sago and cook till it turns clear and thick. Mix in the rest of the above ingredients and form wafers as shown in the recipe entitled Cabbage Wafers. They should be fried in the same way as cabbage wafers.

Rice Wafers

2 cups rice flour. 3 tblsps. sago. 1 tblsp. poppy seeds. 1 tsp. cumin seeds. Salt to taste.

Boil 4 cups water and put in sago. When the sago turns clear add the rest of the above ingredients. Cook over a slow fire till the mixture turns thick. Remove from fire and make wafers as shown in the recipe entitled Cabbage Wafers. They are fried in the same way as Cabbage Wafers.

Wheat Wafers

½ kilo wheat. 1 tblsp. each of cumin and sesame seeds. 50 grams ground green chillies. Salt to suite the taste. Soak wheat in the water for 3 days continuously, changing the water daily. Drain out the water after 3 days and grind to a very smooth and fine paste. Strain the paste through a cloth and place the strained milk in a vessel. Cook over a slow fire till the mixture turns thick, stirring all the time. Remove from fire and make wafers as shown in the recipe entitled Cabbage wafers. They are fried in the same way as Cabbage Wafers.

Potato Wafers

Peel and cut potatoes into thin wafers with the help of a sharp knife. Boil water, add salt and potatoes, boil for a second and remove from the fire. Strain out the water completely and scatter on a cloth. Dry in the sun nicely and store in airtight containers. These wafers too are fried like cabbage wafers. You can also make wafers out of sweet potatoes and tapioca in the same way.

Banana stem murukku

1 foot fine variety banana stem. 1 kilo rice flour. 25 grams ground green chillies. 1 tsp. turmeric powder. Salt to taste. Mince the stem of bananas finely and then put in a kilo of water and boil till done. Put in the rice flour and keep on stirring till the mixture turns thick. Mix in the above ingredients and remove from fire. Cool a little and put a little mixture at a time either in a "Murukku", "Chakuli", or "oralu", mould and squeeze out on a plastic sheet. Dry as shown in cabbage wafers. They are fried like cabbage wafers.

Wheat Murruku

½ kilo wheat. 1 tblsp. sesame and cumin seeds. 50 grams ground green chillies. Salt to taste.

Prepare the batter as shown in the recipe entitled wheat wafers, then put the batter either in murruku, chakuli or oralu mould and squeeze on a plastic sheet. Dry thoroughly as shown in cabbage wafers. They too are fried in the same way as cabbage wafers.

Rice papadams

1 kilo rice. 25 grams gingelly seeds. 25 grams ground green chillies. Salt to taste.

Soak rice whole night in water. Next morning, drain out the water and grind it to a thick paste. Mix in the rest of the above ingredients and spread the mixture in small and thin round shapes on plaintain leaves. Steam for 10 minutes. Remove from fire, cool and then place in the sun for a few days to dry completely. Store in airtight containers. They are fried in the same way as cabbage wafers.

Papadam

1 kilo urad dal flour. 50 grams each of papad soda and salt. 25 grams each of coarsely pounded peppercorns and red chillies. Salt to taste.

Heat half kilo water and put in soda and salt. When the soda and salt dissolves completely into the water remove from fire. Cool and strain through a cloth. Keep 100 grams of flour aside and in the remainder mix in all the spices. Then add enough cooled water to form a stiff dough. Cover and set aside whole night. Next morning, pound the dough till very smooth. Divide into lime-sized balls. Dip each ball in oil and roll it out as thinly as you can with the help of a little dry flour. Place them in the hot sun for a few days till they turn completely dry and store in airtight tins. When wanted for use either bake them on open fire or a hot girdle or fry them like cabbage wafers.

Maida papad

500 grams refined flour or maida. 1 tblsp. each of cumin seeds and chilli powder. Salt to taste.

Mix together all the above ingredients with enough water to form a thin batter then cook over a slow fire till the mixture turns into a thick paste. Remove from fire, cool till bearably hot and then spread into a thin round circle on a plastic sheet. Dry nicely in the sun and store in airtight tin. When wanted for use fry like cabbage wafers.

Jackfruit papad

Select mature but unripe jackfruit, remove peels and seeds and cut into pieces. Steam till cooked then cool and then add salt and chilli powder and pound till a firm dough is obtained. Form into balls and flatten them on greased banana leaves and dry nicely in the sun. They are fried like cabbage wafers.

VEGETABLE DISHES

Stuffed brinjals

250 grams small brinjals. 1 tsp. each of urad and channa dal. ¼ coconut, finely grated. ½ tsp. turmeric powder. 4 red chillies. 5 peppercorns. 1 tsp. coriander seeds. ½ tsp. til or sesame seeds. Salt to taste.

Fry all the above things with the exception of brinjals and turmeric to a red colour and then grind to a coarse paste. Wash and cut the brinjals into fours halfway through. Mix salt and turmeric in the paste and stuff into the brinjals. Heat 4 tblsps. oil and put in the brinjals, sprinkle left-over masala over top. Cover tightly and cook without adding water till the brinjals are done.

Brinjal kootu

500 grams small brinjals. ½ cup toovar dal. 1 tblsp. grated coconut. ½ tsp. turmeric powder. 1 tsp. each of urad dal, coriander and mustard seeds. 1 lime-sized ball of tamarind. 4 peppercorns. 6 red chillies. A pinch of asafoetida. A few curry leaves. ½ tsp. urad dal. Salt to suit the taste.

Cover tamarind in water for 5 minutes, then squeeze out the juice. Cut the brinjals into four halfway through. Cook the dal till soft. Fry coconut, remaining dals, red chillies, pepper and coriander seeds to a red colour and grind to a paste. Put brinjals to cook with tamarind, salt and turmeric. When the brinjals are almost done, put in the ground paste and dal. When the brinjals turn tender remove from fire. Heat 1 tblsp. oil and put in asafoetida, curry leaves and mustard seeds. When the seeds stop popping, remove from fire and put into the kootu. Serve hot.

Brinjal curry

500 grams brinjals cut into pieces. 5 red chillies. 1 tblsp coriander seeds. 1 tsp. channa dal. 1 tsp. sesame seeds or til. A pinch of asafoetida. 1 lime-sized ball of tamarind.

½ tsp. turmeric powder. ¼ coconut, grated. A few curry leaves. Salt to taste. 1 tsp. mustard seeds.

Fry chillies, coriander, dal, coconut and til in a little oil to a red colour and grind to a coarse paste. Cover tamarind in water for 5 minutes then squeeze out the pulp. Heat 2 tblsps. oil and put in the mustard and turmeric powder. When the seeds stop popping, put in the brinjals, curry leaves and salt. Fry until the brinjals start changing colour. put in the tamarind water and cook till almost done. Put in the ground paste and continue cooking till the brinjals are tender. Remove from fire and serve hot.

Bagaru Baigan. (Hyderabad)

250 grams small brinjals. 1 lime-sized ball of tamarind. 25 grams finely grated jaggery. 100 grams onions. 1-inch piece ginger. 4 flakes garlic. 2 red and 3 green chillies. ½ tsp. turmeric powder. ¼ dry coconut. 1 tblsp. each of coriander, cumin and til seeds. 12 cashewnuts. Salt to taste.

Cover tamarind with water for 5 minutes, then squeeze out the juice. Wash and cut the brinjals into fours halfway through. Grind together ginger, garlic, chillies and handful of coriander leaves. Roast the whole onions on fire till the skin turns black, remove the peel and grind the onions to a paste. Roast coconut, coriander, cumin and til till red and grind with coconut to a paste. Mix jaggery in tamarind and set aside till the jaggery dissolves. Mix together all the above ingredients with the exception of tamarind and stuff the mixture liberally into the brinjals. Heat 4 tblsps. oil and toss in ¼ tsp. cumin seeds. When the seeds stop bursting, add the brinjals and cook till the brinjals are tender. Add tamarind and continue cooking till the gravy turns thick and the oil floats to the top. Serve immediately.

Brinjal Sambhar

500 grams small brinjals. 1 lime-sized ball of tamarind. 100 grams toovar dal. 1 medium onion, finely sliced. 1

tsp. turmeric powder. 1 tblsp. coriander seeds. 6 red chillies. 4 tblsps. grated coconut. 1 tsp. each of fenugreek seeds, peppercorns, cumin seeds, channa dal and mustard seeds. A pinch of asafoetida. 4 cardamoms. A few curry leaves. Handful of coriander leaves.

Cover tamarind with water and squeeze out the pulp when it turns soft. Fry 4 chillies, coconut, coriander, fenugreek and cumin seeds, cardamoms and channa dal till red and grind to a paste. Wash and soak the dal for 2 hours in water, then put it to cook in the water in which it was soaked along with salt and turmeric. When the dal turns half tender, cut the brinjals into four halfway through and toss in. Cook till the brinjals are almost done, then put in the tamarind, ground paste and coriander leaves. Remove from fire when both the dal and brinjals are done. Heat 2 tblsps. oil and put in asafoetida, mustard seeds and curry leaves and remaining red chillies. When the seeds stop popping, put in the onions and fry to a pale golden colour. Put the mixture into the sambhar and serve hot.

Vaingya ambot (Mangalore)

250 grams brinjals, diced. 100 grams toovar dal. 1 lime-sized ball of tamarind. 2 medium onions, minced. 1 small onion, cut into fine rings. ¼ coconut. 6 red chillies. ½ tsp. turmeric powder. 1 tblsp. coriander powder. A pinch of asafoetida. 1 tsp. mustard seeds. Salt to suit the taste.

Cover tamarind with water for 5 minutes, then squeeze out the pulp. Roast coconut and chillies and grind to a paste. Wash and soak dal in water for 2 hours, then put the dal to cook in the water in which it was soaked along with turmeric and salt. When the dal is half cooked add minced onions and brinjals and contniue cooking till the vegetable is almost done. Put in the ground paste, tamarind and coriander powder. Remove from fire when both the brinjals and the dal is cooked. Heat 2 tblsp. oil and put in asafoetida and mustard seeds, when the seeds stop crackling, put in the sliced onion and fry to a pale golden colour. Put into the ambot and serve hot.

Banana erussery (Kerala)

4 large raw bananas. ½ tsp. turmeric powder. ½ coconut.
½ tsp. mustard seeds. 1 tsp. cumin seeds. A few curry
leaves. 2 flakes garlic. crushed. 2 red chillies. 1 small
onion, finely sliced. Salt to taste.

Boil bananas in water after peeling them to which salt
and turmeric powder has been added till soft and dry.
Grind ¼ coconut, cumin seeds and curry leaves to a paste.
Grate the remaining coconut. Mix the ground coconut
into the bananas and heat the vegetable. Remove from
fire and set aside. Heat 2 tblsps. coconut oil and toss in
mustard, garlic and chillies. When the seeds stop popping,
put in the onion and grated coconut. When the mixture
turns nearly brown, remove from heat and put into the
erussery. Mix well and serve hot.

Stuffed bananas

4 big raw bananas, peeled. ¼ coconut, grated. 4 green chillies. Handful of coriander leaves. ½ tsp. mustard seeds.
2 red chillies. ½ tsp. turmeric powder. Salt and lime juice
to taste.

Cut the bananas into 2-inch pieces lengthwise. Cut each
piece into half halfway down the centre. Grind together
coconut, green chillies and coriander leaves. Mix in salt,
turmeric and lime juice and stuff the paste into the bananas. Heat 1 tblsp. oil and put in mustard seeds and red
chillies. When the seeds stop popping, put in the bananas.
Cover tightly and cook till the bananas are done. Serve
hot.

Banana kut (Kerala)

1 cup channa dal. 2 raw bananas, peeled and diced. 1
lime-sized ball of tamarind. ½ coconut, grated. 4 red chillies, diced. ½ tsp. turmeric powder. A few curry leaves.
½ tsp. each of urad dal and mustard seeds. Salt to taste.

Cover tamarind with wtaer for 5 minutes, then squeeze
out the pulp. Grind together coconut and 3 red chillies.

Wash and soak dal in 3 cups water for a few hours. Then put it to cook in the water in which it was soaked along with turmeric and salt. When the dal is half cooked, add the bananas. Cook till the dal is almost done, then put in the ground paste and tamarind. When the dal is done, remove from fire. Heat 1 tblsp. oil and put in urad, mustard, curry leaves and the remaining chilli. When the mixture turns brown, put into the vegetable. Serve immediately.

Banana Thoran (Kerala)

2 big raw bananas peeled and diced. ¼ coconut, grated. 2 green chillies. 2 small onions. ½ tsp. turmeric powder. 2 flakes garlic. ¼ tsp. cumin seeds. A few curry leaves. ½ tsp. mustard seeds. Salt to taste.

Grind coarsely coconut, chillies, onion and garlic. Powder cumin seeds. Cook bananas in little water along with salt till tender and dry. Add coconut and curry leaves and mix nicely. Cook on a slow fire for 5 minutes and remove from fire. Heat 1 tblsp. oil and put in the mustard seeds, when the seeds stop bursting, put into the thoran and serve hot.

Carrot Kosumali (Mangalore)

2 medium carrots. A couple of tender leaves of cabbage. ¼ tsp. mustard seeds. ¼ tsp. turmeric powder. Handful of coriander leaves. Salt, lime juice and chilli powder to taste.

Grate carrots and cabbage finely. Heat 1 tsp. oil and put in all the above ingredients with the exception of carrots, cabbage and coriander leaves. When the mustard stops bursting, put into the carrots. Mix well and serve decorated with coriander.

Cauliflower Kootu

1 medium cauliflower, broken into flowerets. 1 cup grated coconut. 2 red chillies. ½ tsp. turmeric powder. 1 tsp. each of urad dal, cumin and mustard seeds. A few curry leaves. Salt to taste.

Grind coconut, cumin seeds and chillies to a paste. Put cauliflower to cook in very little water along with salt and turmeric powder. When the cauliflower is almost done, put in the ground paste. Remove from fire when the cauliflower turns soft. Heat 1 tblsp. oil and put in mustard, dal and curry leaves. When the mixture turns almost red, put into the kootu. Serve hot.

Cabbage Fried

1 medium cabbage, finely grated. 1 tsp. each of mustard and urad dal. 2 red chillies. A few curry leaves. ¼ tsp. turmeric powder. 2 tblsps. grated coconut. Handful of sliced corriander leaves. Salt to taste.

Heat 1 tblsp. oil and put in mustard, dal and chillies and fry till the dal turns red. Add turmeric and curry leaves and fry briefly. Put in the cabbage and salt. Cover tightly and cook over a slow fire without adding water till it is done. Serve garnished with coconut and corriander leaves.

Cabbage and Peas Mulagotal (Kerala)

100 grams toovar dal. 1 cup finely grated cabbage. 100 grams shelled green peas. 1 carrot, grated. 1 drumstick, scraped and cut into small pieces. 4 red chillies. ½ coconut, grated. ½ tsp. mustard seeds. 1 tsp. urad dal. ½ tsp. turmeric powder. A few curry leaves. Salt to taste.

Grind coconut and chillies to a slight coarse paste. Wash and soak dal in water for a few hours. Then place the dal to cook in the water in which it was soaked along with salt and turmeric powder. When the dal is half cooked, add all the vegetables. Cook till the vegetables are almost done. Put in the coconut paste and remove from fire when the vegetables and dal both turn soft. Heat 2 tblsp. oil and put in the urad dal and mustard seeds, when the dal turns red, add curry leaves fry briefly and put over the mulagottal. Serve piping hot.

Drumstick Curry (Mangalore)

4 drumsticks, scraped and cut into small pieces. 100 grams toovar dal. 1 lime-sized ball of tamarind. 4 red chillies.

1 tblsp. corriander seeds. 6 peppercorns. ½ tsp. turmeric powder. ¼ tsp. anise seeds. 1 tsp. poppy seeds. ¼ coconut, grated. 6 flakes garlic, sliced. ½ tsp. cumin seeds. A few curry leaves. Salt to taste.

Cover tamarind with water for 5 minutes, then squeeze out the pulp. Roast chillies, peppercorns, corriander, anise, poppy and cumin seeds and coconut and grind to a coarse paste. Wash and soak dal in water for a few hours, then place it to cook in the water in which it was soaked along with salt and turmeric powder. When the dal is half cooked, add drumsticks and continue cooking till the dal and the drumsticks are almost tender. Put in the tamarind and ground paste. Mix well and remove from fire when the vegetable is done. Heat 2 tblsps. of oil and fry garlic and curry leaves to a light golden colour. Put into the curry and serve hot.

Drumstick Flower Treat

250 grams drumstick flowers, cleaned. 1 big onion, minced. 4 green chillies, minced. 1 medium tomatoe, diced. 1 cup thick coconut milk. ½ tsp. turmeric powder cloves. 2 cardamoms. A small piece cinnamon stick. 1 tsp. cumin seeds. Handful of corriander leaves. Salt to taste.

Powder together all the spices. Heat 1 tblsp. oil and toss in the onions and chillies. Fry till soft. Add all the spices, fry briefly then add the tomatoe and salt. When the tomatoe turns soft, put in the flowers, mix well, then add the coconut milk. Cover tightly and cook till tender and dry. Serve hot garnished with corriander leaves.

Drumstick Sambhar

100 grams toovar dal. 2 drumsticks, scraped and cut into big pieces. 2 red and 2 green chillies. 1 lime-sized ball of tamarind. 1 tsp. each of mustard and fenugreek seeds. A pinch of asafoetida. Few curry leaves. Handful of corriander leaves. ½ tsp.. turmeric powder. Sambhar masala . . . . ½ tsp. til. ½ tsp. cumin seeds. 1 tsp. each of channa dal and fenugreek seeds. ½ tsp. mustard seeds. 4 red chillies.

Roast all the ingredients of sambhar masala till red, then grind to a fine powder. Wash and soak dal in water for a few hours. Then put the dal to cook in the water in which it was soaked. Add turmeric and salt and when soft, remove from fire, mash to a paste with a wooden spoon and pass through a sieve. Cover tamarind with water for 5 minutes then squeeze out the pulp. Heat 2 tblsps. oil and put in the mustard and fenugreek seeds and asafoetida. When the seeds turn red, add drumsticks and sambhar masala and mix nicely. Pour in tamarind water, 1 cup water and curry leaves and salt. When the drumsticks are almost cooked, mix in the dal. Continue cooking till the drumsticks are done. Serve garnished with corriander leaves.

Jackfruit Curry (Kerala)

1 medium raw jackfruit. 1 coconut, grated. 1 medium onion. 1 small onion, finely sliced. 6 green chillies. ¼ tsp. turmeric powder. A few curry leaves. 1 tsp. cumin seeds. 1 tsp. mustard seeds. Salt to suit the taste.

Peel the jackfruit. Grease your hands and separate the fruit. Remove seeds and cut into pieces. Grind to a paste medium onion, chillies and cumin seeds. Grind coconut coarsely. Put the fruit in a pan along with salt and turmeric and very little water. Cover tightly and cook over a slow fire till almost done. Put in the ground paste and curry leaves and continue cooking till the fruit is done. Remove from fire and set aside. Heat 1 tblsp. of oil and put in the mustard seeds, when they stop popping, add the sliced onion and fry to a pale golden colour. Put into the fruit and serve at once.

Jackfruit Seed Curry

25 seeds of jackfruit. 3 cups coconut milk. 4 green chillies, slitted. 2 medium onions. 1 tsp. each of turmeric powder and ground cumin seeds. 1 tblsp. corriander powder. 1 tsp. rice. 1 tblsp. grated coconut. Salt and chilli powder to taste.

Roast the rice and grated coconut along with 4 red chillies and grind to a paste. Grind onions separately. Wash and boil the seeds till their jackets burst, then mash lightly. Heat 1 tblsp. oil and put in onions and fry till soft. Add all the spices and fry briefly. Put in the seeds slitted chillies and salt and coconut milk, bring to a boil, reduce heat to simmering and put in the ground paste. Cook till the gravy turns a little thick. Serve garnished with sliced corriander leaves.

Ginger Curry (Kerala)

25 grams ginger. 2 green chillies. A big piece of coconut. 1 lime-sized ball of tamarind. 1 tblsp. grated jaggery. 4 red chillies. A few curry leaves. ½ tsp. fenugreek seeds. ¼ tsp. mustard seeds. Salt to taste.

Cover tamarind with water for 5 minutes, then squeeze out the pulp. Roast and powder red chillies and fenugreek seeds. Peel and slice ginger, chillies and coconut finely. Add very little water and salt and cook over a slow fire till the ginger turns soft and dry. Heat 2 tblsps. coconut oil and put in the mustard, when it stops crackling, toss in the ginger mixture and fry till it turns golden. Put in the ground spices, tamarind and jaggery and cook till the gravy turns a little thick. Serve piping hot.

Potato kut (Kerala)

250 grams potatoes, peeled: ½ tsp. fenugreek seed 8 red chillies. 1 tsp. mustard seeds. A few pods tamarind. A pinch of asafoetida. Handful of sliced corriander leaves. Salt to taste.

Roast mustard and fenugreek seeds, chillies and asafoetida and grind to a thick and fine paste with tamarind. Cut potatoes into fine straws and deep fry till they start changing colour. Drain, cool, mix in salt and deep fry once again till crisp and golden. Drain thoroughly and mix in the ground tamarind paste. Serve immediately garnished with corriander leaves.

Pineapple pachadi (Kerala)

1 ripe pineapple. 250 grams grated jaggery. A few curry leaves. 5 red chillies. 1 coconut, grated. ½ tsp. turmeric powder. ½ tsp. mustard seeds. 1 tsp. cumin seeds. Salt to taste.

Peel the pineapple. Cut out all the eyes carefully. Cut into slices. Remove the inside hard portion and dice. Grind coconut, cumin and mustard seeds into a paste. Grind red chillies separately. Boil pineapple in little water to which turmeric, chilli powder and salt has been added. When the pineapple turns tender, put in the jaggery and keep on stirring till it turns into a syrup. Put in the coconut paste and curry leaves. Mix well and remove from fire. Put in 2 tblsps. coconut oil before serving.

Pineapple kalan (Kerala)

1 ripe pineapple. 4 red chillies. ¼ tsp. each of mustard and fenugreek seeds. 3 red chillies, broken. A few curry leaves. 1 glass butter milk. ½ tsp. turmeric powder. ½ coconut, grated. 1 small onion. 1 tsp. cumin seeds. Salt to taste.

Peel the pineapple, remove all eyes carefully and cut into slices. Remove the inside hard portion and dice into pieces. Grind to a paste coconut, cumin seeds and green chillies. Place pineapple, salt and turmeric powder in a pan with very little water. Cover tightly and cook till the pineapple is almost done. Pour in the butter milk and add the ground paste. Continue cooking till the pineapple is tender. Mix in the curry leaves and remove from fire. Heat 2 tblsps. coconut oil and toss in the mustard and fenugreek seeds and red chillies. When the mixture turns brown put into the kalan and serve immediately.

Papaya masala

1 medium raw papaya. 6 green chillies, minced. 1 tsp. urad dal. ½ tsp. turmeric powder. 2 tblsps. grated coconut. ½ tsp. mustard seeds. Handful of sliced corriander leaves. Salt to taste.

Peel and cut the papaya into small pieces. Heat 2 tblsps. oil and add dal and mustard. When the mixture turns red, add turmeric, fry briefly and put in papaya, salt and chillies. Cover tightly and cook without adding water till the papaya is done. Serve garnished with coconut and corriander leaves.

Papaya kootu

1 raw papaya. 1 lime-sized ball of tamarind. 2 small onions. 4 red chillies. 2 tblsps. grated coconut. 25 grams fried groundnuts. 1 tblsp. urad dal. 1 tblsp. corriander seeds. $\frac{1}{2}$ tsp. cumin seeds. $\frac{1}{2}$ tsp. turmeric powder. Salt to taste.

Peel and dice papaya into pieces. Cover the tamarind with 1 cup water for 5 minutes, then squeeze out the pulp. Fry the rest of the ingredients with the exception of groundnuts to a red colour and grind to a paste along with the nuts. Boil papaya in tamarind water till almost done. Mix in the rest of the above ingredients and continue cooking till done. Serve garnished with sliced corriander leaves.

Papaya curry

1 raw papaya. 1 medium onion, finely sliced. 4 green chillies, slitted. 4 flakes garlic. 1-inch piece ginger. 1 tsp. cumin seeds. 4 red chillies. 5 peppercorns. A few curry leaves. $\frac{1}{2}$ coconut. $\frac{1}{4}$ tsp. turmeric powder. 1 big tomato, peeled and sliced. Salt to taste.

Peel and cut the papaya into pieces. Grind coconut, peppercorns, red chillies, garlic and ginger and cumin seeds to a paste. Heat 2 tblsps. of oil and fry the onions lightly. Put in the ground paste and turmeric and salt and fry till nicely browned and a nice aroma comes out of it. Put in the papaya. Mix well, put in the tomato and 2 cups water and cook till the papaya is done. Mix in the curry leaves and remove from fire. Serve hot.

Mango curry (Kerala)

3 raw mangoes. 8 red chillies. $\frac{1}{2}$ tsp. each of fenugreek and mustard seeds. A big pinch asafoetida. A few curry leaves. 1 tsp. powdered cumin seeds. Salt to taste.

Peel and slice mangoes. Roast red chillies and fenugreek seeds and powder. Mix powdered spices and salt with mangoes and put in 3 cups water. When the mangoes turn soft, put in the curry leaves and remove from fire. Heat 1 tblsp. of coconut oil and put in mustard and asafoetida. When the seeds stop popping, put into the curry and serve immediately.

Mango curry no. 2

3 raw mangoes, peeled and sliced. A few pods tamarind. 1 cup coconut milk. 5 red chillies. $\frac{1}{2}$ tsp. turmeric powder. 1 medium onion, finely sliced. A few curry leaves. 1 tsp. ground cumin seeds. Salt to taste. Jaggery if desired.

Grind tamarind and chillies to a paste. Heat 1 tblsp. of oil and fry onion till it starts changing colour. Add ground paste and fry nicely. Put in the mangoes, salt, turmeric and ground cumin seeds and mix well. Pour in coconut milk and cook till the mangoes are done. Mix in jaggery and curry leaves and remove from fire. Serve hot.

Potato curry (Andhra Pradesh)

250 grams potatoes. 100 grams, sliced onions. $\frac{1}{2}$ tsp. each of mustard and cumin seeds and turmeric powder. A few curry leaves. 2 flakes garlic, sliced. 4 red chillies, powdered. Salt to taste. 1 cup milk.

Heat 2 tblsps. oil and put in the mustard and cumin seeds and curry leaves. When the seeds stop popping, put in the onions and garlic and fry till light golden colour. Add all the spices and fry briefly. Then put in peeled and sliced potatoes and salt. Fry for a few minutes. Pour in milk and cook over a slow fire till the potatoes are tender and almost dry. Serve hot garnished with corriander leaves.

Potato Song (Mangalore)

500 grams potatoes, boiled and peeled and cubed. 50 grams onions, sliced. 10 red chillies. 1 lime-sized ball of tamarind. Handful of sliced corriander leaves. Salt to taste.

Grind chillies and tamarind to a paste. Heat 3 tblsps. oil and fry onions to a pale golden colour. Add tamarind mixture and fry for a few minutes. Put in the potatoes and salt and fry for 5 minutes stirring all the time. Serve garnished with corriander leaves.

Potato fried

250 grams potatoes, boiled, peeled and diced. 1 tsp. mustard seeds. 1 tsp. urad dal. A pinch of asafoetida. 2 red and 2 green chillies. 2 tblsps. grated coconut. Handful of sliced corriander leaves. Salt to taste.

Heat 2 tblsps. oil and put in asafoetida, chillies, urad dal and mustard. When the dal turns red, add potatoes and salt and fry till the potatoes turn red. Serve hot garnished with coconut and corriander leaves.

Cluster bean kootu

250 grams cluster beans or gavar. ½ coconut, grated. 3 red chillies. 5 peppercorns. 1 tsp. urad dal. A pinch of asafoetida. A few curry leaves. ½ tsp. cumin seeds. 100 grams toovar dal. ½ tsp. turmeric powder. Salt to taste.

Wash and soak the dal in water for a couple of hours, then place it to cook in the water in which it was soaked after adding salt and turmeric powder till the dal turns soft. Remove from fire and set aside. Dice the beans and steam them till tender. Heat 1 tblsp. oil and put in red chillies, peppercorns, urad dal and asafoetida and fry till red. Remove from fire and grind to a paste along with coconut. Reheat the dal and mix in the beans, curry leaves and coconut paste. Simmer on a gentle fire for 5 minutes and remove from fire. Heat 1 tblsp. of oil and put in the cumin seeds, when they stop popping, put into the dal and serve hot.

Cluster bean with dal

250 grams cluster beans, diced. 1 cup moong dal. ½ coconut, grated. 3 red chillies, diced. ½ tsp. turmeric powder. Handful of corriander leaves. 1 tsp. mustard seeds. Salt to taste.

Wash and soak the dal in 3 cups water for 1 hour. Heat 1 tblsp. oil and put in the mustard and chillies. When the mustard stops bursting, add beans, turmeric and salt. Mix well then pour in the dal along with the water in which it was soaked. Cover tightly and cook till the beans and the dal are almost cooked. Add coconut and continue cooking till the vegetbale is done. Serve garnished with corriander leaves.

Ladies finger pachadi (Kerala)

12 ladies fingers. 1 lime-sized ball of tamarind. 4 green and 1 red chilli. ½ tsp. sugar. A few curry leaves. Pinch of asafoetida. ¼ tsp. each of mustard seeds and turmeric powder. Salt to taste.

Cut the cone-shaped heads of ladies fingers and the tip ends, then dice into pieces. Cover tamarind with 1 cup water for 5 minutes, then squeeze out the pulp. Heat 1 tblsp. oil and put in mustard, red chilli and asafoetida. When the seeds stop popping, add the ladies fingers, curry leaves and green chillies. Fry till the vegetable starts changing colour, then add the rest of the ingredients. Cook over a slow fire till the vegetable is done and the gravy thick.

Mango pachadi

2 big raw mangoes, peeled and sliced. For pods of tamarind. 50 grams grated jaggery. ½ tsp. mustard seeds. Few neem flowers. 1 tsp. rice flour. 4 red chillies, broken. A few curry leaves. Salt to taste.

Fry the flowers in oil till crisp. Drain, cool and powder them finely. Cover the tamarind with water for 5 minutes, then squeeze out the pulp. Heat 2 tblsps. oil and put in the chillies, curry leaves and mustard seeds. When the seeds stop crackling, put in the pieces of mango and fry briefly. Put in tamarind and salt and cook till the mango is almost done. Add jaggery and stir till it dissolves. Mix in rice flour dissolved in 1 tblsp. water and powdered flowers. Cook till thick. Remove from fire and serve either hot or cold.

Mangai Chundal

250 grams dried green peas. 1 large raw mango, peeled and sliced. 1 medium onion, sliced. ¼ coconut finely grated. 4 red and 2 green chillies, diced. 1 tsp. mustard seeds. A few curry leaves. ½ tsp. turmeric powder. 1 tblsp. finely sliced coconut. Handful of sliced corriander leaves. Salt to taste.

Fry the sliced coconut to a golden colour and set aside. Wash and soak the peas whole night in water. Next morning, add a pinch of soda and boil them in the water in which they were soaked till tender. Drain out the water and set the peas aside. Heat 2 tblsps. oil and put in the mustard seeds. When they stop bursting, add onion, chillies and curry leaves and cook till the onions turn soft. Put in the turmeric and salt and fry briefly. Add mangoes and grated coconut. Cover tightly and cook till the mango is done. Put in the boiled peas. Mix well and keep on stirring for 5 minutes continuously. Serve garnished with fried coconut and corriander leaves.

Tomato curry

2 large tomatoes, peeled and sliced. 1 tblsp. grated coconut. A few curry leaves. 2 cups thick coconut milk. ¼ tsp. mustard seeds. ½ tsp. turmeric powder. 4 green chillies, slitted. ¼ tsp. corriander seeds. 1-inch piece ginger. 1 medium onion. Salt and chilli powder to taste.

Grind coconut, corriander seeds and ginger to a paste. Heat 1 tblsp. oil and put in the mustard seeds, when the seeds stop popping, add the onion and ground coconut paste and fry to a golden colour. Put in turmeric and chilli powder and salt and fry briefly. Add tomatoes and cook till soft. Pour in the coconut milk. Mix well and add curry leaves and chillies. Cook over a slow fire for 10 minutes. Serve hot with plain boiled rice.

Methi bhaji curry

1 bunch fenugreek leaves, cleaned and sliced. 3 cups buttermilk. ½ tsp. mustard seeds. ¼ tsp. fenugreek seeds. 2 tsps. gram flour. ½ tsp. turmeric powder. 1 big onion, minced. 3 green chillies, minced. 1-inch piece ginger, minced. Salt and chilli powder to taste.

Heat 1 tblsp. oil and add fenugreek and mustard seeds. When the seeds stop popping, add ginger, onion and chillies and fry till soft. Add fenugreek leaves, turmeric, salt and chilli powder. Cover tightly and cook till the leaves are almost done. Mix gram flour in buttermilk and pour in. Continue cooking till the bhaji is cooked and the gravy a little thick. Serve hot.

Methi and dal curry

1 cup cooked toovar dal. 2 bunches fenugreek leaves, cleaned and sliced. 1 cup finely grated coconut. ½ tsp. mustard seeds. ½ tsp. turmeric powder. Salt to suit the taste. 4 red chillies, broken.

Heat 2 tblsps. oil and put in the chillies and mustard When the mustard stops popping, add leaves, salt and turmeric and cover tightly and cook till the leaves are almost done. Put in the dal and coconut and continue cooking till the leaves are tender. Serve hot.

Hyderabadi chilli curry

24 thick and large green chillies, slitted. 4 flakes garlic. 1-inch piece ginger. 2 tblsps. sesame seeds. 25 raw peanuts. 1 tsp. cumin seeds. 1 tblsp. corriander seeds. 1 lime-sized ball of tamarind. 2 medium onions. Salt and chilli powder to taste. ½ tsp. turmeric powder.

Roast til, cumin and corriander seeds and powder them. Grind peanuts coarsely. Cover tamarind with 2 cups water and squeeze out the pulp after 5 minutes. Grind ginger, garlic and onion separately to a paste. Heat 2 tblsps. oil and fry the onion paste to a light golden colour. Add peanuts and powdered spices and fry nicely. Put in the chillies and fry till they start turning brown. Pour in tamarind water and cook till the gravy turns a little thick. Serve hot.

Methi bhajee sambhar

1 bunch fenugreek leaves, cleaned and sliced. 1 lime-sized ball of tamarind. ½ tsp. mustard seeds. 1 tsp. urad. 2 tsps. channa dal. ¼ tsp. fenugreek seeds. ¼ tsp. turmeric powder. 1 tsp. rice flour. 2 red chillies, broken. A few curry leaves. Pinch of asafoetida. Sambhar masala . . . . see recipe entitled Drumstick Sambhar.

Cover tamarind with 2 cups water for 5 minutes, then squeeze out the pulp. Heat 2 tblsps. oil and put in the mustard and fenugreek seeds, dals, asafoetida, sambhar masala, and chillies. When the dals turn red, add fenugreek leaves and fry till dry. Add curry leaves, salt, chilli powder and turmeric. Mix well and then add tamarind water. Cover and cook till the leaves are almost done, then mix the rice flour in 2 tblsps. water and put in. Cook till the leaves are tender and serve hot with plain boiled rice.

Vegetable sambhar

100 grams toovar dal. 50 grams ladies fingers. 1 brinjal. 1 potato. 1 drumstick. 8 peeled baby onions. 2 medium tomatoes, peeled and sliced. 5 red chillies. 6 green chillies, slitted. 1 lime-sized ball of tamarind. A pinch of asafoetida. 1 tsp. turmeric powder. 1 tblsp. corriander seeds. 2 big onions, sliced finely. A few curry leaves. ½ tsp. each of mustard and cumin seeds. Salt to suit the taste.

Roast and powder corriander seeds, red chillies, asafoetida and fenugreek seeds. Cover tamarind with 2 cups water and squeeze out the pulp after 5 minutes. Wash dal and soak in water for 1 hour, then cook it in water in which it was soaked after adding turmeric and salt till it turns soft. Remove from fire, mash to a paste with the help of a wooden spoon and pass through a sieve. Cut the cone-shaped heads and tail-ends of ladies fingers. Slit them halfway through in the centre and set them aside. Peel and dice potatoes and drumsticks. Also slice the brinjals. Heat 4 tblsps. oil and fry the sliced onions till soft. Add tomatoes, turmeric and salt and cook till the tomatoes turn soft. Add, all the vegetables with the exception of ladies fingers. Mix nicely and put in the powdered masala. Cook till the vegetables are almost done, then put in the ladies fingers. When the vegetables turn tender, add the dal and mix well. Put in the chillies and bring to a boil, reduce heat and simmer gently for 5 to 7 minutes. Remove from fire and set aside. Heat 2 tblsps. oil and put in the curry leaves and mustard and cumin seeds. When the seeds stop popping, put into the sambhar and serve immediately. Sambhar has quite a lot of gravy just like curry therefore add as much water as you like to the dal when you add it to the vegetables. Sambhar is eaten with plain boiled rice.

Bittergourd ghashi (Mangalore)

2 bittergourds. 1 lime-sized ball of tamarind. ¾ cup finely grated coconut. 5 red chillies. 1 tsp. urad dal. 2 tsps. corriander seeds. ¼ tsp. turmeric powder. ¼ tsp. mustard seeds. A few curry leaves. 2 tblsps. grated jaggery. Salt to taste.

Cut bittergourds into thin rings. Roast dal, corriander, Methi seeds and grind to a paste with coconut and chillies. Cover tamarind with 2 cups water for 5 minutes and squeeze out the pulp. Heat 1 tblsp. oil and put in bitter-gourds, jaggery, salt and turmeric. Cook till half done, put in ground masala and remove from fire when it is cooked. Season with mustard and curry leaves.

Plain sambhar

1 cup toovar dal. 1 big onion, finely sliced. 100 grams shelled green peas. 4 red chillies. 1 tsp. corriander seeds. 5 peppercorns. 1 lime-sized ball of tamarind. A pinch of

asafoetida. ½ tsp. each of mustard, cumin and fenugreek seeds. A few curry leaves. Salt to suit the taste

Boil the peas. Cover tamarind with water and squeeze the pulp after 5 minutes. Roast chillies, peppercorns, fenugreek and cumin seeds and powder them finely. Wash and soak the dal in 4 cups water for 15 minutes, then put it to boil in the water in which it was soaked after adding turmeric and salt. When the dal turns soft, remove from fire, mash to a pulp and pass through a sieve. Heat 2 tblsps. oil and fry the onions to a pale golden colour add all the powdered spices and fry briefly, put in the dal, tamarind water and peas, bring to a boil, reduce heat and simmer on a gentle fire for 5 minutes. Remove from fire and set aside. Heat 1 tblsp. oil and fry mustard, curry leaves and 2 broken red chillies till the seeds stop popping and then put into the sambhar. This sambhar goes very well with idli and medhu vada.

Rasam

1 cup toovar dal. 1 lime-sized ball of tamarind. Handful of sliced corriander leaves. A pinch of asafoetida. 3 red chillies. 1 tsp. cumin seeds. 1 tblsp. corriander seeds. 6 peppercorns. 2 flakes garlic. A few curry leaves. ½ tsp. each of mustard seeds and turmeric powder. Salt to taste. Cover tamarind with 1 cup water for 5 minutes, then squeeze out the pulp. Wash and soak dal for 15 minutes in 5 cups water. Roast and powder 2 red chillies, asafoetida, corriander and cumin seeds and peppercorns. Put the dal to cook in the water in which it was soaked along with turmeric till soft. Remove from fire, mash to a pulp and pass through a sieve. Reheat the dal and add the tamarind and powdered spices and salt. Bring to a boil, reduce heat to simmering and cook for 5 minutes. Remove from fire and set aside. Heat 2 tblsps. oil and toss in whole red chilli, curry leaves, garlic and mustard. When the mustard stops bursting and the garlic turns pink, pour into the rasam. Serve immediately.

Tomato rasam

½ cup toovar dal. 4 medium tomatoes, blanched and sliced. ½ tsp. turmeric powder. 1 lime-sized ball of tamarind. A few curry leaves. A big handful of sliced corriander leaves. A pinch asafoetida. ½ tsp. mustard seeds. 1 tsp. cumin seeds. 4 green chillies, slitted. ¼ tsp. urad dal. 2 red chillies, broken. Salt to taste.

Cover tamarind with water for 5 minutes and then squeeze out the pulp. Wash and soak dal in 3 cups water for 1 hour, then put it to cook in the water in which it was soaked along with salt and turmeric powder. When the dal turns soft, mash and pass through a sieve. Add 2 cups more water to dal and put in tomatoes, green chillies, curry and corriander leaves. Cook over a slow fire till the tomatoes turn soft, then put in the tamarind water and cook till the gravy turns a little thick. Remove from fire and keep aside. Heat 2 tblsps. oil and add asafoetida, red chillies, cumin and mustard seeds and urad dal. When the dal turns red put into the rasam. Serve hot.

Avial (Kerala)

50 grams each of brinjals, potatoes, pumpkin and carrots. 1 raw banana. 1 drumstick. 50 grams french beans. 50 grams shredded cabbage. ½ grated coconut. 5 green chillies, minced. ½ cup sour curds. 1 tblsp. roasted cumin seeds. A few curry leaves. ½ tsp. turmeric powder. Salt to suit the taste.

Peel and cut all the vegetables into 1-inch pieces. Grind together coconut and cumin seeds to a very fine paste and blend with the curds. Add salt, chillies and turmeric to vegetables and very little water. Cover tightly and cook over a gentle fire till the vegetables are done. Mix in the coconut paste and mix well. Bring slowly to a boil and put in 1 tblsp. fresh coconut oil and curry leaves. Mix thoroughly and remove from fire.

Tamarind rasam

1 lime-sized ball of tamarind. ½ tsp. peppercorns. 1 tsp. cumin seeds. 1 tblsp. corriander seeds. 1½ tsps. mustard

seeds. 6 flakes garlic. ½ tsp. turmeric powder. A few curry leaves. 4 red chillies. Handful of sliced corriander leaves. Salt to taste.

Grind to a paste cumin, corriander, peppercorns, 4 flakes garlic, 3 red chillies and 1 tsp. mustard seeds. Soak tamarind in 4 cups water for 5 minutes, then squeeze out the pulp. Heat the tamarind water and put in the salt, turmeric, ground paste and corriander and curry leaves. Boil till the rasam begins to froth and remove from fire. Heat 1 tblsp. oil and put in the remaining mustard seeds, garlic and chillies. When the seeds stop bursting put into the rasam and serve hot.

Pepper rasam

10 peppercorns. 2 red chillies. 1 tblsp. corriander seeds. ½ tsp. cumin seeds. 4 flakes garlic. 1 small onion. ½ small onion, finely sliced. ½ tsp. poppy seeds. ½ tsp. turmeric powder. A pinch ajwain. ¼ tsp. mustard seeds. A few curry leaves. 1 lime-sized ball of tamarind. Salt to taste.

Cover tamarind with 4 cups water for 5 minutes, then squeeze out the pulp. Grind together the rest of the above ingredients to a paste with the exception of curry leaves, half onion and 1 red chilli. Heat the tamarind and put in the ground paste. When the rasam begins to froth remove from fire. Heat 1 tblsp. oil and add remaining onion, chilli and curry leaves. When the onion turns pale golden colour put into the rasam. Serve piping hot.

Sweet potato curry

250 grams sweet potatoes. 1 medium onion, minced. 3 green chillies, minced. 2 big tomatoes, sliced. ½ tsp. turmeric powder. ½ coconut, grated. 1 tsp. cumin seeds. 1 tblsp. corriander seeds. 3 flakes garlic. A few curry leaves. 4 red chillies. Handful of sliced corriander leaves. Salt to taste.

Grind to a fine paste coconut, red chillies, garlic, cumin and corriander seeds. Heat 1 tblsp. oil and fry the onions and green chillies till soft. Add tomatoes, turmeric and salt and cook till the tomatoes turn soft. Put in peeled and sliced sweet potatoes and ground paste and cook for 5 minutes. Put in 2 cups water and the remaining ingredients and cook till the vegetable is done. Serve hot.

Savoury sweet potatoes

100 grams sweet potatoes, peeled and finely grated. $\frac{1}{2}$ coconut, finely grated. 4 green chillies, minced. $\frac{1}{2}$ tsp. turmeric powder. 1 tsp. urad dal. $\frac{1}{2}$ tsp. each of cumin and mustard seeds. 2 red chillies, broken. A few curry leaves. 4 flakes garlic. Handful of sliced corriander leaves. Salt and lime juice to taste.

Put the sweet potatoes to cook in a little water along with salt and turmeric powder. When the sweet potatoes are almost done add coconut, green chillies and curry leaves. Remove from fire when the vegetable is done. Heat 2 tblsps. oil and toss in mustard, cumin, red chillies and garlic. When the garlic turns pink and the seeds stop popping, put into the prepared vegetable. Sprinkle on top lime juice and corriander leaves before serving.

Saaru (Mysore)

$\frac{1}{2}$ cup toovar dal. 1 lime-sized ball of tamarind. $\frac{1}{2}$ tsp. mustard seeds. A few curry leaves. A big handful of sliced corriander leaves. 4 red chillies. 1 tsp. corriander seeds. $\frac{1}{2}$ tsp. channa dal. A pinch asafoetida. 1 small piece dry coconut. 1 tsp. cumin seeds. Salt to taste. $\frac{1}{2}$ tsp. turmeric powder.

Cover tamarind with 1 cup water for 5 minutes, then squeeze out the pulp. Roast and grind chillies, coconut, channa dal, asafoetida, corriander and cumin seeds to a paste. Wash and soak dal in 4 cups water for 1 hour, then put it to boil in the water in which it was soaked after adding to it turmeric and salt. When the dal is almost done, put in the tamarind, curry leaves and ground paste. Remove from fire when the dal is done. Heat 2 tblsps. oil and put in the mustard seeds. When they stop bursting, put into the saaru. Serve garnished with corriander leaves.

Moru kolumbu (Kerala)

5 cups buttermilk. $\frac{1}{2}$ coconut, grated. 1 tblsp. cumin seeds. 1-inch piece ginger. 4 green chillies, slitted. 4 red chillies. 1 tblsp. gram flour. $\frac{1}{2}$ tsp. turmeric powder. A pinch asafoetida. 50 grams each of potatoes, pumpkin, french beans. 1 drumstick. 1 raw banana. A few curry leaves. 1 tsp. each of mustard seeds and urad dal. Salt to taste.

Peel and cut all the vegetables in 1-inch pieces. Grind coconut, cumin seeds, ginger and red chillies to a paste. Blend gramflour into buttermilk. Add salt and turmeric into the vegetables with very little water and cook till almost done. Put in the ground paste and continue cooking till the vegetables are done. Pour in buttermilk and bring slowly to a boil. Remove from fire and set aside. Heat 2 tblsps. oil and toss in mustard seeds, dal and curry leaves. When the dal turns red, put into the kolumbu. Serve hot.

Dal curry

250 grams toovar. 1-inch piece ginger. 6 green chillies. 5 flakes garlic. A big handful of corriander leaves. 3 medium onions, minced. Salt and lime juice to taste.

For curry . . . . 1 lime-sized ball of tamarind. 4 red chillies. 1 tblsp. corriander seeds. $\frac{1}{2}$ tsp. turmeric powder. A few curry leaves. 2 medium onions. 2 big tomatoes, blanched and sliced. 4 flakes garlic. A big pinch each of mustard and cumin seeds. $\frac{1}{4}$ coconut. Handful of sliced corriander leaves. Salt to taste.

Soak the dal in water for a couple of hours. Drain and grind to a coarse paste with ginger, chillies, garlic and onions. Mix in the salt, lime juice and corriander leaves and put in a greased thali about half an inch thick. Level the surface and steam till set or a toothpick inserted in the centre comes out clean. Remove, cut into small square pieces and deep fry till golden brown coloured. Drain and set aside. Grind coconut, chillies, corriander seeds and garlic to a paste. Heat 2 tblsps. oil and fry the ground paste nicely. Add tomatoes, salt and turmeric powder and cook till the tomatoes turn soft. In the meanwhile soak tamarind in 4 cups water for 5 minutes and squeeze out the pulp. Pour the tamarind water into the soft toma-toes and boil for 5 minutes, reduce heat to simmering and put in the fried dal pieces. Simmer on a gentle fire for 5 minutes and remove from fire. Heat 2 tblsps. oil and toss in curry leaves, mustard and cumin seeds and 2 broken red chillies. When the seeds stop popping, put into the curry. Sprinkle corriander leaves on top before serving.

Dal kofta curry

1 cup toovar dal. ½-inch piece ginger. 4 green chillies. 2 flakes garlic. 1 small onion. A big handful of corriander leaves.

For curry . . . . 4 cups buttermilk. 4 green chillies, slitted. ¼ coconut, grated. 1-inch piece ginger. 1 tsp. each of cor-riander and cumin seeds and channa dal. ¼ tsp. fenugreek seeds. A few curry leaves. Handful of sliced corriander leaves. ½ tsp. turmeric powder. Salt to taste. ½ tsp. mus-tard seeds.

Wash and soak dal for a few hours. Drain out the water and grind to a coarse paste along with ginger, garlic, chil-lies and onion. Mix in the salt and corriander leaves. Form into small balls and steam for about 20 minutes. Remove from fire and set aside. Grind dal, coconut, cor-riander, cumin and fenugreek seeds to a fine paste. Mix the buttermilk along with ground paste, turmeric and salt. Place the buttermilk on fire and put in the green chillies, bring slowly to a boil and put in the dal koftas. Mix nicely and remove from fire. Heat 2 tblsps. oil and put in the mustard seeds and curry leaves. When the seeds stop bursting, put into the curry. Serve hot garnished with sliced corriander leaves.

Vadai korma

2 cups channa dal. ½ small bunch cleaned and finely sliced fenugreek leaves. 4 small onions, minced. 4 green chillies, minced. 2 flakes garlic, minced. Salt to taste.

For curry . . . . 2 cups thick and 3 cups thin coconut milk. 4 flakes garlic. 1 tblsp. poppy seeds. ½ tsp. turmeric powder. A few curry leaves. Handful of sliced corriander leaves. 2 cardamoms. 8 peppercorns. 2 red chillies broken. 2 green chillies, minced. 2 cloves. 4 small onions, minced. 25 grams each of fried cashewnuts and raisins. Salt to taste.

Wash and soak dal for 1 hour, then drain and grind it to a coarse paste. Mix in fenugreek leaves, onions, chillies and garlic and salt. Form into small round vadas with a hole in the centre on a wet cloth and deep fry the vadas to a golden brown colour. Drain and set aside. Grind garlic, poppy seeds, cardamoms, peppercorns and cloves to a paste. Heat 4 tblsps. oil and fry onions, chillies and curry leaves till golden. Put in the ground paste and fry till the oil floats to the top. Put in the turmeric and salt and fry briefly. Pour in thin coconut milk and bring it slowly to a boil, reduce heat add the vadas and simmer gently for 5 minutes. Pour in thick coconut milk, heat to simmering and remove from fire. Serve garnished with cashewnuts, raisins and corriander leaves.

Vadai curry

250 grams sour curds. 7 green chillies, slitted. 1 small bunch corriander leaves. 1 tsp. each of cumin and mustard seeds. 1-inch piece ginger. 1 tsp. turmeric powder. 1 tblsp. urad dal. 2 tblsps. grated coconut. Salt to taste.

For vadais . . . . 250 grams toovar dal. 1 coconut, finely grated. 10 green chillies. 1 small bunch corriander leaves. 1-inch piece ginger. 1 small onion. Salt to taste.

Wash and soak dal for a few hours in water. Drain out the water and grind to a coarse paste. Mince together the rest of the vadai ingredients and mix into the dal along with salt. Form the mixture into round vadais and steam nicely till done. Remove and set aside. Soak urad dal for a few minutes, drain water and grind to a paste along with the rest of the above ingredients with the exception of chillies. Beat curds nicely with 2 cups water till smooth. Heat 4 tblsps. oil and fry the ground paste till oil starts separating. Put in the turmeric powder and salt and fry briefly, pour in the curds and chillies and if you like a few curry leaves. Bring slowly to a boil, reduce heat and put in the vadais. Simmer on a gentle fire for 5 to 7 minutes. Remove from fire and serve garnished with sliced corriander leaves.

Togari gashi (Mysore)

250 grams whole toovar. 1 coconut, grated. 125 grams cashewnuts. 4 red chillies. ¼ tsp. cumin seeds. 2 tblsps. corriander seeds. 1½ small onions. 2 flakes garlic. ½ tsp. turmeric powder. Salt to taste.

Fry in 1 tblsp. oil corriander, cumin seeds and chillies till red. Also fry coconut, garlic and 1 onion and grind to a paste. Wash and soak dal in water for 4 hours. Soak cashewnuts in water for 1 hour. Drain out the water and set aside. Boil the dal in the water in which it was soaked after adding to it turmeric till the dal is half done. Put in salt and cashewnuts and continue cooking till the dal is almost done. Put in the ground paste and continue cooking till the dal is tender and quite thick. Slice the remaining half onion finely and fry in a little oil till crisp and red, put into the dal and serve hot.

Mixed vegetable treat

125 grams each of sweet potatoes, potatoes and carrot. 100 grams sprouted green grams boiled. 25 grams boiled groundnuts. ½ coconut, finely grated. 4 green chillies, minced. 1-inch piece ginger, minced. ½ tsp. each of mustard seeds, urad and channa dal. A few curry leaves. ½ tsp. turmeric powder. Handful of corriander leaves. 2 red chillies, broken. Salt, sugar and lime juice to taste.

Grate all the vegetables finely Crush the groundnuts coarsely. Heat 4 tblsps. oil and put in the mustard seeds, curry leaves, red chillies and the dals. When the dals turn red, add curry leaves, ginger, green chillies, all but 1 tblsp. coconut and all the vegetables. Fry for 5 minutes, then cover the vegetables with 2 cups water. Cover and cook till the vegetables are almost done. Put in groundnuts, sprouted grams, sugar and salt and continue cooking till the vegetables are done and gravy very thick. Remove from fire and sprinkle on top remaining coconut, corriander leaves and lime juice before serving.

Sago baath

1 cup sago. 2 cups beaten curds. 4 green chillies, minced. 1-inch piece ginger, minced. 1 tsp. mustard seeds. A pinch asafoetida. A few curry leaves. Salt to taste.

Wash the sago and soak in 2 cups water for 15 minutes, then cook in the water in which it was soaked till soft. Heat 1 tsp. oil and put in the mustard seeds and asafoetida, when they stop popping, add chillies, ginger and curry leaves and cook till soft. Mix with curds along with salt and sago. Serve the baath cold. Instead of sago you can also use broken wheat to make this baath.

Coconut kofta curry (Hyderabad)

½ kilo tomatoes, peeled, depiped and pureed. 1 tsp. poppy seeds. 4 cloves. 4 cardamoms. 1 tsp. cumin seeds. 1-inch piece cinnamon stick. 1 small piece dry coconut. 4 red chillies. 1 tsp. turmeric powder. 4 flakes garlic. 1-inch piece ginger. 1 big onion, minced. Handful of finely sliced corriander leaves. A few fried cashewnuts.

For koftas . . . . 1 big coconut. 3 tblsps. gram flour. 8 green chillies. 1 large bunch corriander leaves. A big handful mint leaves. 1 medium onion. 6 flakes garlic. 1-inch piece ginger. 4 ground red chillies. 1 tblsp. garam masala. Salt to taste.

Grind the coconut coarsely and then mix with all the kofta ingredients after slicing them finely. Form the mixture to a smooth dough. Make small balls out of the dough and deep fry in ghee to a golden brown colour. Drain and keep aside. Grind together all the remaining spices, dry coconut, ginger and garlic to a smooth paste. Heat 3 tblsps. oil and fry the onions and ground paste together till the oil separates. Put in turmeric and salt and fry briefly. Add tomatoes and cook till soft. Put in 1 glass of water and bring to boil, boil gently for 10 minutes, put in the prepared koftas and boil for another 5 minutes. Remove from fire and serve hot garnished with cashewnuts and corriander leaves.

Vadai kootukari (Kerala)

3 medium onions, sliced finely. 250 grams peeled baby potatoes. 1 cup thick and 2 cups thin coconut milk. 5 peppercorns. 3 red chillies. 2 cloves. ½-inch piece cinnamon stick. ½ tsp. each of cumin and corriander seeds. 1 bay leaf. ½ tsp. turmeric powder. 1-inch piece ginger. 2 green chillies. A few curry leaves. 1 tblsp. mustard seeds. 1 cup urad dal. Salt to suit the taste.

Roast and powder together all the whole spices with the exception of mustard seeds. Heat 2 tblsps. oil and brown onions and ginger. Add potatoes and fry for 5 minutes. Put in slitted green chillies and thin milk and all the spices and cook till the potatoes are done. Put in thick milk, heat to simmering and remove from fire. Soak dal for a few hours in water, drain and grind to a paste. Add salt and drop with the help of a teaspoon in oil and deep fry to a golden colour, drain and put into the curry. Heat 2 tblsps. oil and put in red chillies, mustard and curry leaves. When the mixture turns brown, pour over the curry and serve hot.

Mysore rasam

1 cup toor dal. 50 grams small tomatoes, quartered. 2 tblsps. tamarind juice. 2 tblsps. corriander seeds. 4 red chillies. 2-inch piece cinnamon stick. 1 tblsp. channa dal. 1 tblsp. coconut. ¼ cup corriander leaves. A few curry leaves. 1 tblsp. powdered jaggery. 1 tsp. each of mustard and cumin seeds. 2 red chillies, broken. Salt to suit the taste. ½ tsp. turmeric powder.

Cook dal in 4 cups water and turmeric powder till soft. Fry together corriander seeds, 4 chillies, cinnamon and channa dal to a red colour and grind to a paste with coconut and corriander leaves. Mash the dal and pass through a sieve. Add 2 cups water, ground paste, curry leaves, jaggery and tomatoes and boil for 15 minutes. Remove from fire and keep it warm. Heat 4 tblsps. ghee and toss in the remaining chillies, cumin and mustard seeds. When the seeds stop popping, put into the rasam and serve hot.

PICKLES AND CHUTNEYS

Mango Kasaundi (Mangalore)

1 kilo raw mangoes. 500 grams til oil. ¾ bottle vinegar. 250 grams sugar. 1 tblsp. fenugreek seeds. 1 tblsp. each of mustard, cumin and corriander seeds. 12 red chillies. 20 flakes garlic. 2-inch piece ginger. 12 green chillies, slitted. A few curry leaves. Salt to suit the taste. 1 tblsp. turmeric powder.

Peel 10 flakes of garlic. Grind to a paste the remaining garlic, red chillies, ginger and all the whole spices. Cut the mangoes into pieces. Apply salt and turmeric powder and set aside whole night. Next morning, drain out the water completely. Heat oil and fry the ground masala nicely. Put in the rest of the ingredients and cook over a slow fire till the mango turns soft. Remove from fire, cool and store in airtight container.

Mango chutney

1 dozen big mangoes. Sugar equal to the weight of mangoes. 12 flakes garlic. 2-inch piece ginger, sliced. 100 grams raisins. 1 cup vinegar. Salt and chilli powder to taste.

Peel, slice and salt the mangoes. Set aside whole night. Next morning drain out the brine and set the mango aside for a couple of hours to turn dry. Put 1 glass of water in sugar and prepare a syrup of one-thread consistency. Add the pieces of mango along with the rest of the ingredients with the exception of raisins and simmer gently till the mango is almost cooked, put in the raisins and continue cooking till the mango is tender. Remove from fire, cool and store in airtight bottle.

Lime pickle

25 limes. 25 big green chillies. 25 1-inch pieces of ginger. Salt equal to the weight of limes. Chilli powder to suit the taste.

Slit the chillies halfway through. Peel the ginger. Deep fry the limes in til oil till golden and soft, drain, cool and cut into four halfway through. Put 2 glasses of water in salt and boil till you find crystals forming at the edge of the water. Remove from fire. Stuff each lime with 1 chilli and 1 piece of ginger and put in a clean jar. Sprinkle on top chilli powder and pour salt water on the whole. Cover tightly and set aside for 15 days, being careful to shake the jar nicely at least once daily.

Hot mango pickle (Andhra Pradesh)

25 green mangoes. 2 cups salt. 250 grams red chillies. Handful of curry leaves. 25 grams each of cumin and mustard seeds and turmeric powder. ½ kilo sweet oil.

Grind all the spices. Cut mangoes into small pieces. Rub salt on them and set aside whole night, next morning, squeeze out all the water from mangoes and set aside to turn dry for at least 4 hours. Put 4 cups of water in 2 cups of salt and boil till you find crystals forming at the edge of the water. Remove from fire. Heat oil till you find blue smoke rising from its surface, lower the flame and put in the ground spices, mix well, add the water and boil for a few minutes. Mix in the mangoes and remove from fire. Remove from fire, cool and bottle.

Sweet potato chutney (Mysore)

250 grams sweet potatoes, boiled and peeled. 2 green mangoes. 4 red chillies. 1 tblsp. urad dal. ¼ tsp. cumin and mustard seeds. A few curry leaves. Salt to taste.

Roast the dal till red and grind to a paste along with mangoes, sweet potatoes, curry leaves and 3 chillies. Heat 1 tsp. oil and mustard and cumin seeds and the remaining chilli till the seeds stop bursting, put over the chutney and serve when cold.

Apple chutney

10 medium apples. ¼ bottle vinegar. 12 flakes garlic, crushed. ½ cup sugar. 1 big piece ginger, crushed. ½ cup

chopped raisins. ½ cup diced dates. 1 tsp. ground cumin seeds. 1 tsp. garam masala. 2 tblsps. chilli powder. Salt to taste.

Peel, slice the apples. Put in a heavy-bottomed dekchi along with all the above ingredients with the exception of raisins, dates and sugar. Cook over a slow fire till the apples turn soft and then put in the remaining ingredients. When the sugar dissolves and the chutney turns thick, remove from fire. Cool nicely and bottle.

Tomato chutney

3 big tomatoes. 4 green chillies, minced. 1 medium onion, minced. ¼ tsp. urad dal. ¼ tsp. mustard seeds. A big pinch of turmeric. Handful of corriander leaves. Salt and chilli powder to taste.

Heat 1 tblsp. oil and put in mustard and dal, when the dal turns red, add the onion and chillies and fry till soft. Put in tomatoes, salt, turmeric and chilli powder and cook till the tomato turns soft and dry. Remove from fire and serve garnished with corriander leaves.

Brinjal chutney (Mysore)

1 big brinjal. 2 green chillies. 1 red chilli. 1 tsp. urad dal. 1 lime-sized ball of tamarind. ½ tsp. grated jaggery. Salt to taste.

Bake the brinjal either on charcoal or gas flame till the skin wrinkles and turns black. Toss into cold water, cool and peel. Heat 1 tblsp. oil and fry red chilli and dal till red. Remove and grind to a fine paste with all the above ingredients. This chutney keeps for a few days.

Chilli chutney

1 bunch corriander leaves. 25 grams green chillies. Juice of a sour lime. Salt to taste.

Grind chillies and corriander to a paste and mix in all the above ingredients.

Coconut chutney

½ coconut, grated. 1-inch piece ginger. ½ bunch corriander leaves. Handful of roasted gram. 4 green chillies. 1 lime-sized ball of tamarind. ½ tsp. each of mustard seeds and urad dal. A few curry leaves. Salt to taste. 1 red chilli broken into bits.

Soak tamarind in half cup water for 5 minutes then squeeze out the pulp. Grind together all the above ingredients to a paste with the exception of dal, mustard seeds, curry leaves and red chilli. Mix the ground paste into the tamarind water, heat 1 tsp. of coconut oil and put in the mustard, dal, red chilli and curry leaves, when the dal turns red, put into the chutney.

Avakkai mangai (Andhra Pradesh)

6 big raw mangoes. 100 grams each of mustard seeds and red chillies. ½ litre gingelly oil. 25 grams turmeric powder. 10 grams each of fenugreek and corriander seeds. Salt to taste.

Wash and cut the mangoes with their seeds into big pieces. Set aside to dry for a couple of hours. Dry all the masala or spices in the sun and powder them. Mix all the spices into the mangoes and put them in a clean jar. Pour oil on the top, mix well and set aside for 15 days before using it, taking care to shake at least once daily.

Hot mango chutney

6 large mangoes. 25 grams chilli powder. 1 tsp. each of fenugreek seeds and turmeric powder. 1 tblsp. mustard seeds. ½ tsp. asafoetida. 250 grams gingelly oil. Salt to taste.

Peel mangoes, discard seed and grind to a paste. Powder fenugreek seeds. Heat oil to smoking, reduce heat and put in the mustard seeds and asafoetida, when the seeds stop bursting, add mangoes, turmeric and salt. Cook over a slow fire till all the moisture is absorbed and the chutney turns thick. Mix in the rest of the ingredients and remove from fire. Bottle when cool. It lasts for a whole year.

Peanut chutney

1 coconut, grated. 25 grams roasted groundnuts. 1 small onion. 4 green chillies. 1-inch piece ginger. Handful of corriander leaves. Salt to taste.

Grind all the above ingredients to a very fine paste without adding water.

Onion Chutney

2 medium onions. 4 green chillies. 3 red chillies. 1-inch piece ginger. 1 lime-sized ball of tamarind. Salt to taste.

Grind all the above ingredients to a very fine paste without adding water.

Corriander chutney

2 bunches corriander leaves. 6 green chillies. ½ tsp. mustard seeds. 1 lime-sized ball of tamarind. Jaggery and salt to suit the taste.

Heat 1 tsp. oil and toss in mustard seeds, when they stop popping, put in chillies and corriander leaves, fry briefly and remove from fire and grind to a fine paste without adding water.

Mint chutney

1 bunch mint. A big handful corriander leaves. 1 tiny onion. 4 green chillies. A little tamarind. ½-inch piece ginger. 1 tsp. each of sugar and lime juice. Salt to taste.

Grind all the above ingredients to a fine paste without adding water.

Drumstick chutney

1 drumstick, boiled. 2 green chillies. A little tamarind. 1 small onion. Handful of corriander leaves. Salt to taste. 1 tiny piece ginger.

Remove the inside pith of the drumstick and grind to a paste with the rest of the above ingredients without adding water.

Dal chutney

½ cup each of urad and gram dal. 1 tsp. each of chilli powder and powdered cumin seeds. ¾ tsp. pepper. ½ tsp. asafoetida. 1½ tsp. salt.

Heat 2 tblsps. oil and fry both the dals to a nice golden colour, add all the spices, mix well, remove from fire, cool, powder and bottle.

Puli thokku

200 grams thick green chillies. 1 ball tamarind. A big pinch asafoetida. ½ tsp. mustard seeds. Salt to taste.

Cover tamarind with hot water for 15 minutes and squeeze out the juice. Slit the chillies. Heat 2 tblsps. oil put in the mustard and asafoetida, when the seeds stop popping, put in the chillies and fry for 2 minutes. Put in the tamarind juice and salt and cook till thick. Remove from fire, cool and put in airtight bottle.

PACHADIES AND SAMBALS

Radish pachadi

1 cup thick curds. 1 tender radish, scraped and grated finely. 2 green chillies. ½ tsp. mustard seeds. Handful of corriander leaves. Salt to taste.

Beat curds well. Mix in the rest of the above ingredients with the exception of mustard seeds. Heat 1 tblsp. ghee and toss in the mustard seeds. When they stop popping, put into the curds. Mix well and serve cold.

Onion pachadi

1 cup thick curds. 1 large onion, peeled and sliced finely. 2 red chillies. Handful of corriander leaves. 1 tblsp. grated coconut. ½ tsp. mustard seeds. Salt to suit the taste.

Grind the coconut and chillies to a paste. Fry onion in little ghee till it turns limp. Mix the onion into the curds with the rest of the above ingredients with the exception of mustard seeds. Heat 1 tblsp. ghee and toss in the mustard seeds, when they stop popping, put into the curds. Mix well and chill before serving.

Potato pachadi

1 cup thick curds. 1 large potato, boiled, peeled and mashed coarsely. 2 green chillies, minced. Handful of corriander leaves. ½ tsp. mustard seeds. ½-inch piece minced ginger. Salt to taste.

Mix all the above ingredients into the curds with the exception of mustard seeds. Fry mustard seeds in 1 tblsp. ghee till they crackle and mix into the pachadi before serving.

Pakodi pachadi

1 cup thick curds. Handful of moong dal. 3 green chillies. Pinch of asafoetida. Handful of corriander leaves. ½-inch piece ginger. ½ tsp. mustard seeds. Salt to taste.

Soak dal in water for a few hours. Drain out the water and grind to a paste with chillies, asafoetida, ginger and salt. Drop teaspoonfuls of batter in smoking ghee and fry the pakodis to a golden colour. Drain nicely and soak in water for 5 minutes. Squeeze out the water and put the pakodis into the curds along with the rest of the above ingredients with the exception of mustard seeds, fry the mustard seeds in a little ghee till they start crackling and put into the pachadi. Mix well before serving.

Tomato pachadi

1 cup thick curds. 1 big tomato, sliced finely. 2 green chillies. 1 tsp. ground mustard seeds. ½ tsp. mustard seeds. Handful of corriander leaves. Salt to suit the taste.

Grind chillies and mix into the curds with the rest of the above ingredients with the exception of ½ tsp. of mustard seeds. Fry the mustard seeds in a little ghee till they pop and put into the pachadi.

Sweet potato pachadi

1 cup beaten curds. 1 big sweet potato, boiled, peeled and diced. 4 green chillies, minced. 1 red chilli, broken into bits. ½ tsp. mustard seeds. Handful of corriander leaves. Salt to taste.

Mix together all the above ingredients with the exception of red chilli and mustard seeds. Fry the chilli and the mustard seeds in a little ghee till they stop popping, then put into the pachadi.

Ladies finger pachadi

1 cup thick curds. 4 large tender ladies fingers, diced into small rounds. ½ tsp. each of urad dal and mustard seeds. 1 red chilli, broken into bits. Handful of corriander leaves. Salt to taste.

Fry ladies fingers in ghee till crisp. Drain and put into the curds with the rest of the above ingredients with the exception of mustard seeds and red chilli. Fry the mustard seeds and chilli in little ghee till the seeds stop popping then mix into the pachadi.

Cauliflower pachadi

1 cup thick curds. ½ cup grated cauliflower. 2 green chillies, minced. ½ tsp. mustard seeds. 1 red chilli. Handful of corriander leaves. Pinch of turmeric powder. Salt to taste.

Heat 1 tblsp. ghee and put in cauliflower. Cover tightly and cook without adding water till done. Mix the cauliflower into the curds along with salt, green chillies, corriander leaves. Break the red chilli into bits then heat ghee and put it in along with turmeric and mustard. When the seeds stop popping, mix into the curds. Serve cold.

Brinjal pachadi

1 cup beaten curds. 1 brinjal. 1 green chilli, minced. ½ tsp. each of mustard and urad dal. 1 red chilli, broken into bits. Handful of corriander leaves. Salt to taste.

Bake the brinjal over a charcoal or gas fire till the skin wrinkles and turns black. Toss into cold water, peel the skin and mash the pulp into a paste. Mix with curds along with salt, green chillies and corriander leaves. Heat 1 tsp. ghee and put in the mustard seeds, dal, red chilli and fry till the seeds stop popping. Mix into the curds and serve cold.

Cucumber pachadi

1 cup beaten curds. 1 small cucumber, finely grated. ½ tsp. mustard seeds. A big handful of finely sliced corriander leaves. 2 green chillies, minced. A pinch asafoetida. Salt to taste.

Mix cucumber with curds along with the rest of the above ingredients with the exception of mustard seeds and asafoetida. Heat 1 tsp. ghee and toss in · asafoetida

and mustard seeds. When the seeds stop crackling mix
into the curds. Serve cold.

Mango pachadi

1 cup beaten curds. 1 big ripe mango. A big pinch each
of mustard and cumin seeds. 1 red chilli, broken into
bits. A few curry leaves. Salt to suit the taste.

Peel and slice the mango. Mix into the curds. Roast and
pound the cumin seeds and mix in along with pepper.
Heat 1 tsp. oil and toss in mustard, chilli and curry leaves.
When the seeds stop popping mix into the curds. Serve
cold. Instead of mango you can also use banana, ripe
pineapple and jackfruit.

Ginger pachadi

1 cup thick curds, beaten. 15 grams ginger. 2 tblsps. grated
coconut. 2 green chillies, minced. A few curry leaves. 1
tsp. mustard seeds. 1 small onion, minced. Salt to taste.

Cook ginger, chillies and half of the onion without adding any water in a airtight vessel till soft. Remove and set
aside. Grind coconut and half of mustard to a paste. Mix
the coconut and ginger into the curds along with salt.
Heat 1 tsp. ghee and add mustard seeds, curry leaves and
remaining onion. When the mustard seeds stop bursting,
remove and mix into the curds. Serve cold garnished with
corriander leaves.

Banana pachadi

1 cup beaten curds. 2 bananas. 2 green chillies, minced.
1 tsp. ground coconut. A pinch of asafoetida. 1/4 tsp. mustard seeds. 1/2 tsp. sugar. A few curry leaves. Salt to taste.
1 red chilli, broken into bits.

Peel the bananas and dice them. Mix them into the
curds along with salt, green chillies and coconut. Heat
1 tsp. oil and put in asafoetida, curry leaves, mustard
and red chilli. When the seeds stop bursting mix into the
curds. Serve cold.

Brinjal sambal

1 big brinjal. ½ cup thick coconut milk. 1 small onion, minced. 1 flake garlic, minced. 2 green chillies, minced. ¼-inch piece ginger minced. 1 tsp. ground cumin seeds. Salt, lime juice and chilli powder to taste.

Roast the brinjal either on a charcoal or gas fire till the skin wrinkles and turns black. Toss into cold water, peel and mash the pulp. Heat 1 tsp. of oil and fry onion, ginger and garlic till soft. Remove from fire and mix into the brinjal with the rest of the above ingredients. Serve cold decorated with coriander leaves.

Prawn sambal

12 prawns, cooked and minced. 1 small onion, minced. 1 flake garlic, minced. ½-inch piece ginger, minced. 3 green chillies, minced. A few sliced curry leaves. 1 tsp. ground cumin seeds. 1 tblsp. finely grated coconut. 4 tblsps. thick coconut milk. Salt, lime juice and chilli powder to taste. Handful of sliced coriander leaves.

Fry onion, garlic, ginger, chillies and curry leaves in 1 tblsp. oil till soft. Mix in the prawns, salt and cumin seeds and remove from fire. Put in the coconut milk and lime juice and chilli powder. Serve cold garnished with grated coconut and coriander leaves.

Potato sambal

1 big potato, boiled, peeled and diced. 4 tblsps. thick coconut milk. 1 small spring onion, minced with a little of the green portion. 2 green chillies, minced. Handful of sliced coriander leaves. 1 tblsp. grated coconut. Salt, chilli powder and lime juice to taste.

Mix together all the above ingredients with the exception of coconut and coriander leaves. Serve cold garnished with grated coconut and coriander leaves.

Onion sambal

1 medium onion, finely sliced. 4 green chillies, minced.
1 small cucumber, finely grated. 4 tblsps. thick coconut.
milk. Lime juice and salt to taste.

Mix together all the above ingredients before serving.

Tomato sambal

1 big tomato, finely sliced. 1 small onion, finely sliced.
1 small cucumber, finely sliced. 2 green chillies, minced.
4 tblsp. thick coconut milk. 1 tsp. grated coconut. A few
sliced coriander leaves. Salt and lime juice to taste.

Mix together all the above ingredients with the exception
of coconut and coriander leaves. Serve garnished with
coriander leaves and coconut.

TEA-TIME SNACKS

Rice dosa

3 cups rice. 1 cup urad dal. 1 tblsp. fenugreek seeds. Salt to suit the taste.

Soak rice and dal and fenugreek seeds separately for 6 hours. Drain and grind to a fine paste separately then mix together. Add salt and set aside whole night. Next morning, pour in enough hot water to form a thick batter. Heat a flat girdle to smoking, lower heat and put in a teaspoon of oil and a pinch of coarse salt, when the salt starts crackling wipe the surface clean. Then once again grease the girdle liberally with oil and pour in 2 tblsps. of batter. Spread the batter into a thin round with the help of a flat spatula. Cover the dosa with a cover for a minute, uncover and sprinkle a little water on top and spread it once again with the back of a katori. When the underside turns golden pour a little oil around the edges and turn over. Remove when both the sides turn golden and serve with coconut chutney while it is still piping hot. After you remove one dosa to facilitate spreading of batter clean the girdle each time by sprinkling a little water and wiping with a small piece of brinjal using the stem as a handle.

Narial dosa

3 cups rice. 1 finely grated coconut. Salt to taste.

Wash and soak rice in water for 6 hours. Drain out the water completely and grind to a very fine paste. Add coconut and grind once again to a fine paste. Mix in salt and set aside for 2 hours. Prepare the dosas as shown in the above recipe. Serve with either butter and honey, butter and sugar or ghee and jaggery or sugar.

Dal dosa (Kerala)

2 cups moon dal. 2 small onions. 4 green chillies. 1 big bunch coriander leaves. Salt to taste.

Wash and soak dal in water for 4 hours. Drain and grind it to a fine paste. Mince together the rest of the above ingredients and mix into the dal along with salt. Set aside for 1 hour, then prepare dosas as shown in the recipe entitled Rice Dosa.

Jaggery dosa

1 cup maida. ½ cup rice flour. ½ cup very finely grated coconut. 1 tsp. ground cardamoms. 1½ cups finely grated jaggery.

Soak jaggery in a little hot water, when it dissolves, strain. Mix together the rest of the above ingredients, then add the jaggery water to make a thick batter. If the batter is not of required consistency, add a little milk or flour to it. Mix well then prepare dosas in the same way as shown in the recipe entitled Rice dosas.

Rava dosa

1 cup rava or semolina. 1 cup maida. ½ cup rice flour. 2 small onions, minced. 1 bunch sliced coriander leaves. 4 green chillies, minced. 1 small piece coconut, finely sliced. A few cashewnuts, chopped finely. Salt to suit the taste.

Mix together all the above ingredients then add enough water to form a thick batter then prepare the dosas as shown in the recipe entitled Rice dosas.

Buttermilk dosa

1 cup each of semolina and maida. 2 green chillies, minced. 1 tsp. mustard seeds. 2 small onions, minced. 1 big bunch sliced coriander leaves. Salt to suit the taste.

Heat 1 tblsp. oil and put in the mustard seeds. When the seeds stop popping, remove from fire and mix in all the above ingredients along with enough buttermilk to form a thick batter. Prepare dosas in the same way as shown in the recipe entitled Rice dosas. Serve piping hot either with coconut or tomato chutney.

Masala idli

250 grams rice. 25 grams black gram dal. ½ coconut. 1 small onion. 2 green chillies. Handful of sliced coriander leaves. A few pieces of tamarind. Salt and chilli powder to taste.

Wash and soak rice and dal separately in water for 6 hours, drain out the water and grind the rice and dal together to a smooth and fine paste. Add the coconut and tamarind and grind once again till smooth. Mix in minced onion, chillies, coriander leaves, salt and chilli powder. Add enough water to form a thick batter. Grease either small round katories or idli katories nicely with ghee or oil and fill the katories about three-quarters full. Steam till the idlis are firm, or until a toothpick or a knife inserted in the centre comes out clean. If a little batter sticks to the knife, steam again till the idlies turn completely solid. Remove and serve hot with seasoned curds.

Coconut idli

2 cups parboiled rice. 1 cup grated coconut. 1 tblsp. each of channa and urad dal. 1 tsp. mustard seeds. 2 green chillies. 1 red chillie, broken. A couple of curry leaves. 1 onion, minced. Salt to taste.

Clean and soak the rice for 6 hours, then grind with coconut to a fine paste. Heat 1 tblsp. oil and put in the mustard seeds and the dals. When the dals turn red, add onion and chillies and curry leaves. When the onion turns soft, remove from fire and mix the mixture into the rice paste. Add enough hot water to form a thick paste then steam as shown in the above recipe.

Sweet idli

½ cup urad dal. ¾ cup semolina or rava. 4 tblsps. finely grated jaggery. A big pinch cooking soda. A big pinch salt. $\frac{1}{2}$ cup finely grated coconut. 1 tsp. cardamom powder. A few cashewnuts and raisins, sliced finely. Milk.

Soak dal in water for 4 hours. Drain out the water and grind to a fine paste. Set aside for 4 hours. Roast rava on a dry girdle till it starts changing colour, then mix with dal along with salt and soda. Add enough milk to form a thick and a smooth batter. Mix in 1 tsp. ghee. Mix together coconut, cardamoms, jaggery, cashewnuts and raisins. Half fill greased katories with batter, spread on top a little of the coconut mixture, then cover with batter nicely and steam as shown in the recipe entitled Masala idli. Serve with hot ghee poured on the top.

Dal and vegetable idli

1 cup toovar dal. $\frac{1}{2}$ cup each of channa and moong dal. 1 small bunch fenugreek leaves. 125 grams shelled peas. 1 carrot. $\frac{1}{2}$ coconut. 1 big bunch coriander leaves. 6 green chillies, minced. 1 onion, minced. $\frac{1}{2}$ tsp. mustard seeds. A pinch of asafoetida. Salt to taste.

Soak the dals for 4 hours and grind a little coarsely after draining out the water. Mince together green chillies, fenugreek and coriander leaves. Grate the coconut and carrot finely. Half-boil the peas and grind coarsely. Mix together dals, vegetables coconut and onion. Heat 1 tblsp. oil and put in mustard seeds and asafoetida, when the seeds stop crackling, put into the dal mixture. Mix well add salt and steam the idlies as shown in the recipe entitled Masala idlies.

Dal idli

1 cup each of mung and urad dal. $\frac{1}{2}$ finely grated coconut. Salt to taste.

Soak both the dals whole night in water, drain out the water and grind to a paste. Also grind coconut finely. Mix both the dals together and salt and set aside for 10 hours. Mix in salt and coconut and steam as shown in the recipe entitled masala idlies. Allow to cool, remove them from the katories nicely and gently with a sharp knife so as not to break them. Cut each idli into half and sandwich the two halves together with any chutney of your choice.

Vegetable idli

1 coconut. 2 cups rice. ¼ cup urad dal. 1 potato. 50 grams shelled green peas. 1 carrot. 25 grams cabbage. ¼ cup channa dal. 1 tsp. cumin seeds. 1 small onion, minced. 1 bunch sliced coriander leaves. 4 green chillies, minced. 2 tblsps. finely grated coconut. A pinch of eating soda. Salt to taste. ½-inch piece ginger.

Steam-cook all the vegetables and mince them. Soak dals and rice in water for 6 hours. Extract thick juice from coconut. Grind rice, dals and ginger and cumin seeds to a paste along with chillies. Mix in all vegetables, coconut, coriander leaves, onion, salt, baking soda and enough coconut milk to form a thick batter. Set aside for 1 hour and then steam as shown in the recipe entitled masala idli.

Stuffed idli

1 cup urad dal. 1 cup rice. A pinch of cooking soda. A big pinch of salt.

For stuffing....1 cup sugar: ½ small finely grated coconut. 25 each of finely sliced cashewnuts, almonds and raisins. 1 tsp. cardamom powder. ¼ tsp. grated nutmeg.

Soak the rice and dal separately for 6 hours. Drain out the water nicely, grind them separately and mix them together. Cover and set to rise in hot place for 3 hours. Mix in salt and soda. Melt the sugar over a slow fire till red. Mix in the rest of the filling ingredients and keep aside. Grease katories nicely, half fill with batter, spread on top coconut mixture and cover with more batter to cover the filling nicely. Steam as shown in the recipe entitled masala idli.

Plain sweet idli

1 cup urad dal. 1 cup rice. ½ cup finely grated jaggery.
1 tsp. cardamom powder. ¼ tsp. finely grated nutmeg.

Soak jaggery in 1 cup water till it dissolves, then strain.
Soak rice and dal separately in water for 6 hours. Drain
out the water and grind separately to a paste. Mix with
jaggery and cover and set in a a hot place for 1 hour
then steam as shown in the recipe entitled Masala Idlies.
Serve with hot ghee poured over the top.

Sago idli

250 grams sago. Curds made of ½ litre milk. 4 green chillies, minced. ¼ tsp. mustard seeds. ½-inch piece minced
ginger. Handful of sliced coriander leaves. Salt to taste.

Fry the sago in a little ghee till it is golden coloured. Heat
1 tblsp. ghee and put in mustard, ginger and chillies.
When the seeds stop popping remove from fire. Mix together curds, sago, salt, ginger mixture and coriander
leaves and set aside for 1 hour then steam in the same
way as shown in the recipe entitled Masala idlies.

Idli sambhar

2 cups rice. 1 cup urad dal. Salt to taste. Pinch of soda.

Wash and soak the rice and dal separately for 6 hours.
Drain and grind rice coarsely and the dal till it is light
and frothy. Mix together rice, dal, soda and little water,
salt and set aside whole night. Steam as shown in the
recipe entitled Masala Idlies. Serve with Sambhar poured
over the top. For Sambhar see chapter on *Vegetable
Dishes.*

Peanut uppama

2 cups fresh and tender peanuts. Handful of sliced coriander leaves. ½ tsp. turmeric powder. ¼ tsp. mustard seeds.
A pinch of asafoetida. ½ coconut, grated finely. 4 green
chillies, minced. 1 large onion, minced. Salt and chilli
powder to suit the taste.

Chop the nuts coarsely. Heat 2 tblsps. ghee and put in the mustard seeds and asafoetida. When the seeds stop popping, put in onion and chillies and fry till brown. Put in turmeric and salt and mix well. Put in nuts and coconut, mix well then pour in 1 cup water. Cover and cook till the nuts are tender and dry. Serve hot garnished with chopped coriander leaves.

Vermecelli uppama

200 grams vermecelli. 1 tsp. urad dal. ½ tsp. mustard seeds. 4 green chillies, minced. 25 grams fried and broken cashewnuts.

Heat 2 tblsps. ghee and fry the vermecelli to a golden colour. Heat 2 tblsp. ghee in a separate pan and put in mustard seeds and dal. When the dal turns red, put in chillies and fry lightly. Add salt and 2 cups water, bring to a boil, reduce heat and put in the vermecelli and keep on stirring frequently till the vermecelli is cooked and thick. Mix in the cashewnuts and remove from fire. Serve hot with coconut chutney.

Poha uppama

250 grams fine poha. 50 grams boiled and shelled green peas. 1 medium onion, minced. ½ tsp. each of urad dal and mustard seeds. 6 green chillies, minced. A few curry leaves. ½ tsp. turmeric powder. Lime juice and salt to suit the taste.

Clean and soak poha in 4 cups water. Heat 1 tblsp. oil and put in the mustard seeds and dal. When the dal turns red, add onion and chillies and curry leaves and fry till the onion turns soft. Add turmeric powder and salt and mix well. Squeeze out the water from poha and put in along with peas. Keep stirring for 5 minutes. Remove from fire and sprinkle on top corriander leaves and lime juice before serving.

Bread uppama

4 slices of bread. ½ cup well-beaten curds. ½ tsp. each of mustard seeds and urad dal. A few curry leaves. Handful

of sliced corriander leaves. 4 green chillies, minced. Salt and chilli powder to taste. ¼ tsp. turmeric powder.

Slice the bread into small pieces and soak into the curds for 5 minutes. Heat 1 tblsp. oil and put in mustard seeds and dal, when the dal turns red, add chillies and curry leaves and fry lightly. Put in bread, salt, chilli and turmeric powder. Mix nicely and thoroughly. Serve immediately garnished with corriander leaves.

Vegetable uppama

250 grams semolina. 2 carrots. 2 potatoes. 50 grams beans. 25 grams peas and cabbage. 6 green chillies, minced. 1-inch piece ginger, minced. 1 tsp. mustard seeds. 2 tsps. each of urad and channa dal. Handful of sliced corriander leaves. A few curry leaves. Salt to suit the taste. 25 grams fried cashewnuts.

Peel and cut all the vegetables into pieces and steam-cook them. Heat 1 tblsp. ghee and fry the semolina to a light golden colour and set aside. Heat 4 tblsps. ghee and put in the mustard seeds and dals. When they turn golden, put in ginger, chillies and curry leaves and fry lightly. Add salt and vegetables and mix well. Put in 4 cups water and bring to a boil and then add fried rava. Lower heat and cook stirring frequently till the mixture turns dry and thick. Mix in cashewnuts and serve garnished with corriander leaves.

Shahi vegetable uppama

250 grams semolina. 2 carrots. 2 potatoes. 50 grams each of beans and shelled green peas. 1 large onion, finely sliced. A few curry leaves. 1 tsp. each of corriander and poppy seeds. 1-inch piece ginger. ½ tsp. garam masala. 250 grams fried cashewnuts. Handful of corriander leaves. ¼ coconut, grated. Salt to taste.

Grind to a paste ginger, poppy seeds, 2 flakes garlic, coconut and half of the fried cashewnuts and 1 small bunch corriander leaves. Broil semolina to a light golden colour. Peel and cut vegetables into small pieces and steam-cook them. In a pan melt 4 tblsps. ghee and put in onion and curry leaves. When the onion turns soft, put in the ground paste and fry till a nice aroma comes out of it. Add vegetables and spices and salt. Mix well, then. pour in 2 cups water, bring to a boil, reduce heat and put in the fried semolina. Keep on stirring till the rava is cooked and thick. Mix in the cashewnuts and remove from fire. Serve garnished with corriander leaves and sprinkle lime juice on top.

Rice uppama

1 cup rice flour. ½ lime-sized ball of tamarind. ¼ tsp. each of mustard seeds and urad dal. A few curry leaves. 2 green chillies, minced. Salt and chilli powder to taste. Handful of corriander leaves.

Soak tamarind in half cup water for 5 minutes, then squeeze out the juice. Mix the rice into the tamarind juice along with enough water to form a thick batter. Heat 2 tblsps. oil and put in the mustard seeds, chillies and curry leaves and dal. When the dal turns red, put in the batter and keep on stirring till the raw smell disappears. Serve hot garnished with corriander leaves.

Wheat uppama

1 cup wheat rava. ½ tsp. mustard seeds and urad dal. A few curry leaves. 25 grams fried cashewnuts. ¼ tsp. turmeric powder. 4 green chillies, minced. Salt to taste.

Heat 2 tblsps. oil and put in mustard seeds, dal and curry leaves. When the dal turns red, put in wheat and fry nicely. Mix in turmeric, salt and chillies, then pour in 3 cups of water. Cook, stirring frequently till the wheat is cooked and all the moisture is absorbed. Mix in cashewnuts and serve at once.

Rice rava uppama

1 cup rice rava. ½ tsp. urad dal. ½ tsp. mustard seeds. A few curry leaves. 4 green chillies, minced. 1 tsp. toovar

dal. 25 grams fried cashewnuts. Handful of corriander
leaves. 1 tblsp. grated coconut. ¼ tsp. turmeric powder.
Lime juice and salt to taste.

Soak dal toovar in water for half an hour. Drain out
water and grind to a paste. Heat 2 tblsps. oil and put in
mustard and urad dal and curry leaves. When the dal
turns red, add chillies and dal paste. Mix nicely, then put
in 3 cups water. Add rice rava after the water starts boiling and cook stirring often till the rice is tender and dry.
Mix in cashewnuts and remove from fire. Sprinkle on top
lime juice and serve hot garnished with corriander leaves
and grated coconut.

Rava uppama

250 grams rava. 6 green chillies, minced. 1 tblsp. curd.
1-inch piece ginger, minced. 2 to 3 small bay leaves. 1 tsp.
each of mustard seeds, urad and channa dal. 25 grams
fried cashewnuts. A few curry leaves. 1 medium onion,
minced. Salt to taste.

Fry rava to a light golden colour in 1 tblsp. ghee. Heat 2
tblsps. oil and put in the mustard seeds and the dals.
When the dals turn red, add ginger, chillies and bay and
curry leaves and onion and fry till soft. Add curds and
mix well. Then pour in 3 cups water. Put in salt and bring
to a boil, reduce heat and add rava. Cook, stirring frequently till the rava turns thick and dry. Mix in cashewnuts and serve immediately with coconut chutney.

Rava adai

250 grams suji. 50 grams rice flour. 1 tblsp. grated coconut. 2 bay leaves, broken into bits. Salt and chilli powder
to taste. Sour buttermilk.

Mix with suji all the above ingredients, then add enough
buttermilk to form a thick batter. Heat a flat girdle,
grease it nicely with ghee and pour in 3 tblsps. batter.
Spread it into a thick round. When the underside turns

golden, pour a little ghee around the edges. When both the sides turn golden and crisp remove from fire and serve immediately.

Amarnath adai

250 grams rice. 100 grams each of channa and toovar dal. 50 grams urad dal. 1 bunch amarnath or chowlai bhajee. ½ coconut, finely grated. 2 green chillies, minced. A few curry leaves. 1 big pinch asafoetida. Salt and chilli powder to taste.

Clean and dice leaves. Wash and soak the rice and dals separately in water. Grind the dals, rice and coconut and chillies coarsely. Set aside for 3 hours then mix in the rest of the above ingredients. Mix together til and coconut oil and ghee in equal quantities and fry the adai in it as shown in the above recipe. Serve immediately with a bowl of seasoned curds.

Jackfruit adai

1 coconut, finely grated. ½ cup finely sliced ripe jackfruit. ½ cup finely grated jaggery. ½ cup refined flour. 1 tsp. cardamom powder.

Mix together coconut, jaggery and cardamoms and 4 tblsps. water and cook over a slow fire till the mixture turns completely thick and dry. Mix in jackfruit and remove from fire. Put enough milk in flour to form a thin batter. Take banana leaves, separate from stems. Cut into big pieces and brush with water and a little oil. On half of the pieces of leaves, spread the batter nicely on one side, and over it spread a layer of jackfruit mixture. Cover with another leaf, pin edges with toothpicks and steam till cooked.

Rava pongal

250 grams rice rava. ½ coconut, finely grated. 1 green chilli. 2 red chillies. ½ tsp. mustard seeds. 1 tsp. urad dal. 25 grams cashewnuts, fried. A few curry leaves. Salt to taste.

Heat 1 tblsp. each of coconut oil and ghee and put in the mustard seeds, dal and curry leaves and chillies. When the dal turns red, add 500 grams water, coconut and salt and bring to a boil, reduce heat and put in the rice rava. Cover and cook, stirring occasionally till the rice turns tender and thick. Serve hot garnished with cashewnuts.

Oothappam

125 grams parboiled rice. 50 grams urad dal. 2 small onions, finely sliced. 4 green chillies, minced. 1-inch piece ginger, minced. ½ small bunch sliced corriander leaves. Salt to taste.

Soak rice and dal separately whole night. Next morning, drain out the water and grind them together and cover and set aside for 24 hours. Mix in the salt and the rest of the ingredients. Heat a girdle to smoking and pour in 1 tblsp. of ghee, then add 2 tblsps. of batter after mixing into it enough water to make it into pouring consistency. Spread the batter into a round and when the underside turns golden, pour a little ghee around its edges and fry nicely on both the sides. Serve immediately with coconut chutney.

Sago vadai

250 grams each of sago and fried groundnuts. ½ cup curds. 2 potatoes, boiled and peeled. 6 green chillies, minced. 1 small bunch of finely sliced corriander leaves. 1 tblsp. finely grated coconut. A few sliced curry leaves. 1 tsp. cumin seeds. Salt to suit the taste.

Wash the sago and soak in very little water for 4 hours. Powder the groundnuts and mix with the rest of the above ingredients. Form small round and flat balls out of the mixture and shallow fry till crisp and golden. Serve piping hot with chutney of choice.

Sago pakoda

100 grams sago. 200 grams nicely beaten curds. 1 tblsp. gram flour. 1 medium onion, minced. 6 green chillies,

minced. 1-inch piece ginger, minced. A pinch of soda. Salt to taste.

Fry sago in a little oil to a golden colour. Put into the curds and set aside for 8 hours. Then grind the mixture to a paste. Mix in the rest of the above ingredients along with 2 tsps. of oil.

Heat enough oil for deep frying to smoking, lower the heat and put the mixture in it with the help of a teaspoon. Deep fry to a golden brown colour. Drain nicely and serve with chutney of your choice.

Carrot vadai

100 grams carrots. 1 tblsp. grated coconut. 2 green chillies, minced. 25 grams coarsely pounded groundnuts. Handful of sliced corriander leaves. ½-inch piece minced ginger. 100 grams gram flour. ½ tsp. turmeric powder. A pinch of cooking soda. ½ tsp. garam masala. Salt and chilli powder to suit the taste.

Grate the carrots and mix into the gram flour along with the rest of the above ingredients. Sprinkle little water to form a stiff batter. Heat 2 tblsps. oil and mix in. Form into round vadai and deep fry till crisp and golden. Serve hot.

Kobi vadai (Mangalore)

¾ cup each of toovar dal and rice. 1 marble-sized ball of tamarind. 3 tblsps. finely grated jaggery. 1 cup shredded cabbage. 3 red chillies. Salt to taste.

Soak dal and rice separately for 5 hours. Drain out the water and grind both together coarsely. Grind tamarind and chillies to a paste and mix with rice mixture along with the rest of the above ingredients. Form into round vadai on a wet cloth and deep fry to golden brown colour. Drain and serve piping hot.

Beetroot vadai (Mysore)

250 grams beetroots. 125 grams channa dal. 25 grams cashewnuts. 1 medium onion, minced. 1 small bunch cor-

riander leaves, finely sliced... 4 green chillies, minced. ½-inch piece ginger, minced. ¼ tsp. garam masala. Salt to suit the taste. A pinch of cooking soda.

Peel and grate beetroots finely. Fry the dal in a little oil to a golden colour and grind to a paste. Fry the cashew-nuts and pound them coarsely. Mix all the above ingredients in a pan with the exception of soda and cook over a slow fire till the moisture is absorbed and the mixture turns thick. Remove from fire, cool, add soda and knead to a smooth paste. Divide the paste into lime-sized balls and form each ball into a round vadai. Deep fry in oil till golden coloured. Drain thoroughly and serve with chutney of your choice.

Marble uppama

1 cup steamed flour. ½ cup finely grated coconut. ½ tsp. mustard seeds. 1 tsp. urad dal. 2 tblsps. roasted and powdered groundnuts. 1 tblsp. channa dal. 1 medium onion, minced. A few curry leaves. Salt and lime juice to suit the taste.

Mix together flour, coconut, groundnuts and salt. Fry the onion and 2 minced green chillies in a little oil till soft and add to the flour. Then add enough water to form a soft dough. Divide the dough into small balls and steam them for 10 minutes. Heat 2 tblsps. oil and put in dals and mustard seeds and curry leaves. When the dals turn red, put in the balls and mix nicely. Remove from fire and sprinkle on top lime juice and corriander leaves before serving.

Dal and carrot uppama

1¼ cup wheat rava. ½ cup sprouted whole moong dal . . . . see helpful hints. ½ cup finely grated carrots. 4 green chillies, minced. 1 small bunch finely sliced corriander leaves. ½-inch piece ginger, minced. ¼ coconut, finely grated. ½ tsp. urad dal. ¼ tsp. mustard seeds. A few curry leaves. Salt to taste. ½ tsp. channa dal.

Heat 4 tblsps. oil and put in mustard seeds, channa and urad dal, when the dals turn red, put in the carrots, curry leaves, sprouted dal, ginger, chillies and corriander leaves and fry for a while. Pour in 2½ cups water. When the water starts boiling, reduce heat and put in the wheat after mixing in it 1 tblsp. oil. Cook till the wheat turns tender and dry. Mix in coconut and remove from fire. Sprinkle lime juice on top and serve immediately.

Medhu vada (Mysore)

250 grams urad dal. 4 green chillies. A pinch of asafoetida. Few curry leaves. Salt to taste.

Soak dal in water for 5 hours. Drain out the water and grind to a paste along with chillies and asafoetida. Mix in sliced curry leaves and salt. Form into round vadas on a vet cloth. Make a hole in the centre and deep fry to a golden brown colour. Drain and serve either with coconut chutney or with sambhar poured over the top.

For sambhar see chapter entitled *Vegetable Dishes*.

Bonda

250 grams urad dal. 2 green chillies. 6 coarsely pounded peppercorns. 1-inch piece ginger, minced. A few curry leaves, sliced. Salt to suit the taste.

Wash and soak dal in water for 5 hours. Drain the water and grind to a paste along with chillies. Mix in the rest of the above ingredients. Heat enough oil for deep frying to smoking, lower heat and drop the paste with the help of a teaspoon in the oil and deep fry to a golden brown colour. Drain nicely and serve hot with chutney of choice.

Ambade (Mangalore)

1 cup each of moong and urad dal. 1 tsp. cumin seeds. 1-inch piece ginger, minced. 3 green chillies, minced. ¼ coconut, cut into small pieces. Salt to taste.

Wash and soak dals in water for 4 hours. Drain out the water and grind to a slightly coarse paste. Mix in the rest of the above ingredients. Form into small round vadas and deep fry to a golden brown colour. Drain nicely and serve with chutney.

Dal pakoda

1 cup moong dal. ½ cup channa dal. 2 tblsps. urad dal. 1 big onion, minced. 4 green chillies, minced. A few sliced curry leaves. 1 tsp. cumin seeds. ¼ coconut, finely sliced. A pinch of soda. Salt to suit the taste.

Soak the dals separately in water for 4 hours. Drain out the water and grind finely. Mix in the rest of the above ingredients. Form into round balls and deep fry to golden colour. Drain and serve with chutney.

Cabbage Cutlets (Mangalore)

½ cup each of urad, moong and channa dal and rice. 1 big onion, minced. 5 green chillies, minced, ½ coconut, finely sliced. A pinch asafoetida. 1 cup shredded cabbage. Salt to taste.

Soak the rice and dals separately for 5 hours. Drain out the water and grind finely. Mix in the rest of the above ingredients and form into round cutlets and deep fry to a golden brown colour. Drain and serve with chutney of choice.

Coconut cake

1 kilo rice flour. 1 coconut, ground finely. Finely grated jaggery to. taste.

Soak jaggery in water. When it dissolves, strain. Mix together rice flour and coconut. Add jaggery water and make soft dough. Take a clean plantain leaf and make a flat cake about half inch thick and six inches in diameter. Cover with other plantain leaf. Heat a girdle to smoking, lower heat and place the plantain leaf covered cake over it. Cook over a slow fire till both the leaves are burnt.

Then remove the leaves and bake the cake on both the sides to a golden colour. Serve with ghee.

Coconut mutlin (Mangalore)

1 kilo rice. 1 coconut. Salt to taste.

Soak rice for 5 hours. Drain out the water and grind to a paste along with coconut. Add salt and make lime-sized balls. Steam till cooked. Serve with ghee and sugar or honey.

Channa vada

250 grams channa dal. 75 grams urad dal. 2 to 3 red chillies. A pinch of asafoetida. 2 small onions. Salt to taste.

Wash and soak dals separately in water for 4 hours. Drain and grind to a slight coarse paste with all the above ingredients with the exception of onions. Add minced onions. Form into round vadas on a wet cloth and deep fry to a golden colour. Drain and serve hot with chutney of choice.

Coconut balls

$\frac{1}{4}$ cup each of channa, urad, toovar and rice. $\frac{1}{2}$ coconut. A big pinch asafoetida. A few curry leaves. 2 to 3 red chillies. Salt to taste.

Grate coconut finely. Soak rice and dals in water for 5 minutes. Drain and grind coarsely with the rest of the above ingredients with the exception of coconut. Mix in the coconut, form into round balls and deep fry to a golden colour. Serve with chutney of choice.

Rava vada

250 grams rava or semolina. $\frac{1}{2}$ coconut, finely grated. 4 green chillies, minced. $\frac{1}{2}$-inch piece ginger, minced. A few curry leaves. 2 tblsps. sour curds. Salt to taste.

Mix all the above ingredients together to form a batter. If the mixture is too thick add a little water to give it the right consistency. Drop teaspoons of batter in hot

oil and deep fry till golden coloured. Drain and serve
with chutney of choice.

Batata Vada

250 grams potatoes, boiled and peeled. 1 small onion,
minced. ¼ tsp. mustard seeds. 1 tsp. urad dal. 2 green
chillies, minced. Handful of corriander leaves. A few
curry leaves, sliced. ¼ tsp. turmeric powder. A pinch
asafoetida. 1½ cups gram flour. Salt and chilli powder
to taste.

Heat 1 tblsp. oil and put in mustard seeds and dal. When
the dal turns red, put in chillies, onion and curry leaves
and cook till soft. Add potatoes, salt, turmeric and corriander leaves. Mix well and remove from fire. Cool and
form into round balls. Mix together gram flour, asafoetida, salt and chilli powder. Put in enough water to form
a thick batter. Dip the balls one by one into the batter
and deep fry to a golden brown colour. Drain and serve
with chutney of choice.

Pakoda

1 cup gram flour. ½ cup rice flour. 4 green chillies,
minced. A few sliced curry leaves. Handful of corriander
leaves. A pinch asafoetida. A pinch cooking soda. 1 tblsp.
oil.

Mix together all the above ingredients with the exception
of oil. Add enough water to form a thick batter, then
mix in the oil and set aside for 15 minutes. In this batter
you can dip any vegetable of your choice like rings of
brinjals, slices of onions or pieces of ribbed gourds and
deep fry to a golden colour. Drain nicely and serve with
any chutney of your choice.

Bajia

½ cup channa dal. ¼ tblsp. rice. ¼ cup toovar dal. A pinch
each of asafoetida and soda. 2 to 3 red chillies. Salt to
taste.

Soak dals and rice in water for 4 hours. Drain out the water and grind with above ingredients to a slight coarse paste. In this paste you can dip any sliced vegetable of your choice and deep fry to a golden colour. Drain and serve hot with chutney of your choice.

Chakali

1 cup channa dal. ½ cup rice. ¼ cup each of moong and toovar dal. 1 tsp. cumin seeds. 2 tblsps. melted ghee. Salt and chilli powder to taste.

Roast rice and dals over a dry girdle till red, then grind to a fine powder. Pass through a fine sieve and mix in the rest of the above ingredients. Put in enough water to form a soft dough. Heat enough oil for deep frying to smoking, lower heat, hold chakali mould on top of the oil and put in a little dough at a time and press the lever. Fry a few chakalis at a time to a golden brown colour. Drain, cool thoroughly and store in airtight container.

Masala vada

250 grams urad dal. 1 tsp. cumin seeds. 4 green chillies, minced. 1-inch piece ginger, minced. A few sliced curry leaves. 1 small onion, minced. 100 grams mixed boiled vegetables like cauliflower, carrots, peas, frenchbeans. A big pinch asafoetida. Salt and chilli powder to suit the taste.

Soak dal for a couple of hours in water. Drain and grind to a smooth and thick paste. Finely slice all the vegetables and mix into the dal along with all the above ingredients. Form into round vadas on a wet cloth and deep fry to a golden brown colour. Drain and serve with chutney of your choice.

Kuzhal

3 cups rice flour. ½ cup flour of urad dal. 1 tsp. each of pepper powder and ground cumin seeds. 2 tblsps. sesame seeds. 1 tblsp. butter. A pinch of asafoetida. Salt to taste.

Mix all the above ingredients together, then mix in enough water to make soft and pliable dough. Heat enough oil for deep frying to smoking, lower heat and then hold a chakali mould or 'Soriya', over the oil, put in a small ball of dough and press the lever. Fry till they become crisp and golden. Drain, cool thoroughly and store in airtight container.

Akki vade (Mysore)

500 grams rice. 125 grams urad dal. 1 tsp. cumin seeds. 4 green chillies. 1 small bunch coriander leaves. Salt to taste.

Clean and wash the rice. Dry in the sun and powder it. Wash and soak the dal in water for a few hours, drain and grind to a smooth and thick paste. Mix dal with rice powder and the rest of the above ingredients. Form into round vadas on a wet cloth and deep fry in oil till they float to the surface. Drain thoroughly and serve piping hot with chutney of choice.

Potato obbattu (Mysore)

250 grams potatoes or sweet potatoes, boiled, peeled and mashed. 250 grams flour. 4 green chillies, minced. Handful of sliced coriander leaves. $\frac{1}{2}$ tsp. turmeric powder. Lime juice and salt to taste.

Mix together all the above ingredients along with 2 tblsps. melted ghee. Add a little water if necessary to form a dough of soft consistency. Divide the dough into lime-sized balls and form each ball into a round disc or chapati over your hand. Put the obattu on a liberally greased and hot girdle. When the underside turns golden coloured, put a little ghee around its edges and turn over. When both the sides turn golden, remove and serve at once.

Savoury balls

2 cups parboiled rice. 1 cup finely grated coconut. $\frac{1}{2}$ tblsp. each of urad and channa dal and mustard seeds. 2 red and 2 green chillies, minced. A few sliced curry leaves.

1 onion, minced. 1-inch piece ginger, minced. Salt to taste.

Soak the rice in water for 6 hours and grind to a paste with coconut. Heat 2 tblsps. oil and put in the dals and mustard seeds. When the dals turn red, add chillies, curry leaves, onion and ginger and fry till soft. Put in the rice paste and cook over a slow fire till the mixture turns thick and starts leaving the sides of the vessel. Remove from fire, cool and form into round balls. Steam them till cooked. Serve hot with chutney of your choice.

Banana flower chips

Peel off the maroon coloured peel of the flowers and mix with thick tamarind juice, salt and chilli powder. Keep aside for 15 minutes, then deep fry in oil till crisp. Drain nicely and serve either hot or cold.

Bread vadai

1 cup gram flour. 4 slices of bread. A pinch asafoetida. 4 minced green chillies. ½ small bunch finely sliced coriander leaves. 1 big onion, minced. Dash of soda. Salt and chilli powder to taste.

Trim the bread and cut into pieces and soak in a little water till soft. Mix the rest of the ingredients with gram flour. Put in the bread pieces along with enough water to form a thick batter. Drop the mixture with the help of a tablespoon in the smoking oil and deep fry to a golden brown colour. Drain thoroughly and serve piping hot.

Paan poley (Mangalore)

200 grams rice. ½ coconut. 2 tblsps. sugar. Salt to taste.

Soak rice in water for about 6 hours. Drain out the water and grind to a very fine paste along with sugar and salt. Add enough hot water to form a thin batter. Smear a smoking flat girdle liberally with oil and pour the paste evenly to make thin dosa. When cooked and the edges look bit brown fold into quarter and remove from fire. This should be served with Rassu. For Rassu take thick juice of 2 coconuts and mix in finely grated jaggery to suit your taste. When the jaggery dissolves, sprinkle on top powdered cardamoms before serving.

Nippittu

1 cup rice flour. ¼ tsp. powdered sugar. 1 tblsp. gingelly seeds. 2 tblsps. each of coarsely powdered roasted groundnuts and grams or channa. Salt and chilli powder to taste.

Mix together flour, salt, sugar and chilli powder along with enough water to form a soft dough. Divide the dough into small balls. Mix together channa, groundnuts and gingelly seeds and spread over a wet cloth. Press both the sides of the ball over the nut mixture so that the nuts stick to both the sides and deep fry in oil till golden coloured. Drain and serve hot or cold.

Beaten rice samosa

125 grams beaten rice. 250 grams refined flour or maida. 1-inch piece ginger, minced. ¼ finely grated coconut. 1 tsp. roasted and powdered cumin seeds. 4 green chillies, minced. A big handful of finely sliced coriander leaves. Ground sugar, lime juice, salt and chilli powder to taste.

Add enough water to flour to form a stiff dough. Soak beaten rice in water for 10 minutes, then squeeze dry. Place on fire with the rest of the above ingredients with the exception of dough. Let it remain on fire for 2 minutes. Remove and divide the dough and beaten rice mixture into equal number of portions. Roll out the dough into a thin round. Put the mixture on one side of the round and fold over to form crescents. Seal and crimp the edges together then deep fry each samosa to a golden brown colour. Drain nicely and serve with any chutney of your choice.

Suran cutlets

250 grams suran. 2 tblsps. gram flour. Handful of sliced coriander leaves. 4 green chillies. 1-inch piece ginger. 1 small onion. 10 cashewnuts, pounded coarsely. Salt to taste.

Boil suran after peeling it in a little water to which lime juice has been added. Drain out the water completely, put in the rest of the ingredients and place over slow fire. Cook till dry and thick. Remove from fire, cool, form into round cutlets and shallow fry to a golden brown colour. Drain and serve with any chutney of your choice.

Banana kababs (Hyderabad)

6 unripe bananas. 100 grams channa dal. 25 grams cashewnuts. 1 tsp. poppy seeds. 2 cloves. 2 cardamoms. A big handful of coriander leaves. 1 small onion. Salt and chilli powder to taste. 1 cup fine bread crumbs.

For filling......4 tblsps. thick curds. 6 green chillies, minced. A few finely sliced coriander leaves. A few sliced mint leaves. Salt to taste.

Mix together all the filling ingredients. Boil together dal and peeled bananas till tender and dry. Grind to a fine paste with the rest of the above ingredients with the exception of bread crumbs. Put the mixture on a slow fire and cook till dry and thick. Divide the banana mixture and filling into equal number of portions after removing it from fire. Make the banana mixture into long kababs around the filling. Roll in crumbs and shallow fry to a golden colour. Drain and serve with chutney of your choice.

RICE DISHES

RICE DISHES

Mutton pullao (Mangalore)

500 grams rice. 1 kilo mutton, cut into serving portions. 2 big onions, minced. 2-inch piece ginger, minced. 4 flakes garlic, minced. 1 medium onion, cut into thin rings. 4 red chillies, broken into bits. 2-inch piece cinnamon stick, broken into bits. 6 cloves. 6 peeled cardamoms. 25 grams each of fried cashewnuts and raisins. Salt to taste.

Wash and soak rice in water for 1 hour. Fry the onion rings till crisp and golden. Cover mutton with hot water and boil till tender. Drain out the stock and set aside. Heat 4 tblsps. ghee and put in the whole spices and chillies. Fry briefly, then put in minced onion, garlic and ginger and fry to a golden colour. Drain out the water from rice and put in. Mix well and then put in the mutton stock along with enough water to stand 1-inch above the level of the rice. When the rice turns almost tender and dry, add the boiled mutton. Cook till the rice turns completely tender and dry. Serve hot garnished with fried onion rings, raisins and cashewnuts.

Chakkarai pongal

500 grams rice. 1 cup moong dal. 1 litre milk. ½ kilo finely grated jaggery. 100 grams ghee. 50 grams each of fried cashewnuts and raisins. 1 tsp. cardamom powder. ½ tsp. grated nutmeg.

Roast dal till light red. Heat ghee and put in rice and dal and milk and cook till both the rice and dal are soft. Add jaggery, nutmeg and cardamom powder and cook over a slow fire till the jaggery is dissolved and absorbed into the rice. Serve hot garnished with nuts and raisins.

Chitrana (Mysore)

2 cups boiled rice. A big handful sliced coriander leaves. 25 grams fried cashewnuts. A few curry leaves. ¼ tsp. turmeric powder. A pinch of asafoetida. Juice of 1 lime.

1 tsp. each of channa and urad dal. ½ tsp. mustard seeds. 2 red and 2 green chillies. Salt and chilli powder to taste.

Heat 2 tblsps. oil and put in mustard seeds, dals and red chillies. When the dals turn red add the rest of the ingredients with the exception of cashewnuts, coriander and rice. Mix well and then add rice and mix it thoroughly with the fried mixture. Serve hot garnished with cashewnuts and coriander leaves.

Chicken pullao

500 grams rice. 1 chicken, disjointed. 4 green onions, finely sliced. 2-inch piece cinnamon stick. broken into bits. 6 cloves. 6 peeled cardamoms. 1 tsp. garam masala. 1 medium onion, cut into thin rings. 2 hard-boiled eggs, shelled and quartered. 25 grams each of fried finely sliced almonds, cashewnuts and raisins. ½ tsp. turmeric powder. Salt to taste.

Fry the onion rings till crisp and golden. Cover chicken with hot water, put in onions, ginger and salt and garam masala and boil till done. Cool and remove chicken from its stock and set aside. Heat 4 tblsps. ghee and put in the whole spices and turmeric and fry briefly. Add rice, mix well and pour in chicken stock along with enough water to stand 1-inch above the level of the rice. Cook till the rice is almost tender and dry. Mix in the nuts and raisins and remove from fire. Take a glass greased flame-proof dish. Cover the bottom with half of the rice. Put on it chicken and cover the whole with remaining rice. Arrange on the top eggs and fried onions and place on a very slow fire and cook for about 10 minutes or until the rice is completely tender and dry. Serve it in the dish itself.

Vegetable pullao

250 grams rice. 125 grams mixed vegetables like carrots, cauliflower, frenchbeans and peas. 1 big onion, finely sliced. 1 tblsp. coriander seeds. ½ tsp. peppercorns. 3 red chillies. ½ tsp. cumin seeds. 1 tblsp. channa dal. A few

curry leaves. 1 inch piece cinnamon stick. 5 cloves. 50 grams each of fried cashewnuts and raisins. Salt to taste. Coarsely powder both cinnamon and cardamoms. In 1 tblsp. ghee fry red chillies, dal, coriander and cumin seeds till the dal turns red. Remove and grind to a paste. Heat 2 tblsps. ghee and put in onion and curry leaves and cinnamon and cloves and fry till the onion turns limp. Put in all the vegetables and salt and cover tightly and cook till the vegetables are half cooked. Put in the rice and enough water to stand 1-inch above the level of the rice. When the rice is almost tender and dry add ground dal paste. When the rice turns completely tender and dry remove from fire and serve hot garnished with cashewnuts and raisins.

Coconut rice

2 cups boiled rice. ¾ cup finely grated coconut. A pinch of asafoetida. A few curry leaves. 50 grams fried cashewnuts. 1 tblsp. channa dal. 1 tsp. urad dal. ½ tsp. mustard seeds. 4 green chillies, minced. 2 red chillies. Salt to taste.

Heat 4 tblsps. coconut oil and put in asafoetida, mustard seeds, dal and red chillies. When the dals turn red, put in coconut and green chillies and curry leaves and fry till the coconut turns red. Put in the rice and mix thoroughly into the coconut mixture. Serve immediately garnished with cashewnuts.

Potato pullao

1 kilo baby potatoes, boiled and peeled. 125 grams each of rice and moon dal. A big pinch asafoetida. A few curry leaves. ½ tsp. turmeric powder. 25 grams fried cashewnuts. Handful of sliced coriander leaves. 2 tblsps. grated coconut. 1 tblsp. channa dal. 3 red chillies. 2 green onions, minced. 4 tblsps. thick tamarind water. 1-inch piece cinnamon stick. 4 cloves. Salt to taste. 1 tsp. each of channa and urad dal.

Fry the potatoes lightly in oil and set aside. Fry separately in oil coriander seeds, red chillies, asafoetida, coconut, cinnamon and cloves and 1 tblsp. channa dal till red and then grind to a paste. Wash and soak rice and moong dal in water for 1 hour. Heat 2 tblsps. oil and put in the remaining dals and fry till red. Add green onions, drained rice and moong dal. Mix well and pour in enough water to stand 1-inch above the level of the rice. When the rice and dal is almost tender and dry add potatoes, tamarind water, powdered spices, salt and curry leaves and cook till the rice is tender. Serve hot garnished with cashewnuts and coriander leaves.

Bisi bela huliyana (Mysore)

1 cup each of rice and toovar dal. 100 grams mixed vegetables like carrots, cabbage, beans, potatoes and peas. 50 grams fried cashewnuts. 1 lime-sized ball of tamarind. Handful of sliced coriander leaves. A few curry leaves. $\frac{1}{2}$ tsp. mustard seeds. 8 red chillies. 1 tblsp. each channa and urad dal. $\frac{1}{2}$ dry coconut, grated finely. 1 tblsp. fenugreek seeds. Salt to taste.

Boil rice and dal separately till done. Steam-cook all the vegetables. Fry in little oil the channa and urad dals, red chillies, asafoetida, fenugreek seeds and coconut. When the mixture turns red, remove from fire and grind coarsely. Cover tamarind with water for 5 minutes and extract thick juice. Heat 2 tblsps. oil and add mustard and curry leaves. When the seeds stop popping, put in the tamarind juice, vegetables coconut mixture and boiled dal and rice. When the mixture turns thick and blends together nicely remove from fire. Serve hot garnished with coriander leaves and cashewnuts.

Mango pullao

250 grams rice. 2 half-ripe mangoes. $\frac{1}{4}$ coconut, finely grated. $\frac{1}{4}$ tsp. turmeric powder. A few curry leaves. 1 tsp. cumin seeds. 3 red chillies. $\frac{1}{2}$ tsp. each of urad dal and mustard seeds. Salt to taste.

Grind cumin seeds, coconut and 2 red chillies to a paste. Wash and soak the rice in water for 1 hour, then drain out the water. Peel and grate the mangoes finely. Heat 500 grams water to boiling and put in the rice, turmeric and salt, when the rice is almost cooked put in mangoes, coconut mixture and 1 tblsp. ghee and continue cooking till the rice turns tender. Remove from fire and set aside. Heat 1 tblsp. ghee and put in remaining chillies, dal, mustard and curry leaves. When the dal turns red, put into the rice and mix well. Cool before serving.

Prawn Pullao

2 cups rice. 3 cups thin coconut milk and 1 cup thick coconut milk. 500 grams big prawns, shelled. 2 medium onions, finely sliced. 4 cloves. 4 cardamoms. 1-inch piece cinnamon stick, broken into bits. 4 flakes garlic, minced. 1-inch piece ginger, minced. ½ tsp. turmeric powder. 1 tsp. garam masala. 2 hard-boiled eggs, shelled and sliced into thick rings. Salt and chilli powder to taste.

Wash and soak rice in water for 1 hour. Take 1 onion and fry it till crisp and golden. Wash the prawns, remove the inside black viens at the back, wash once again and apply salt, chilli powder, turmeric and garam masala. Set aside for 5 minutes then deep fry till crisp and golden. Drain and set aside. Heat 1 tblsp. ghee and put in whole spices, fry briefly and then add remaining onion, ginger and garlic and fry till soft. Add turmeric, salt and drained rice and then pour in thin coconut milk. Bring to a boil, reduce heat and cook till almost all the moisture is absorbed, then pour in boiling thick coconut milk and prawns and continue cooking till the rice is tender and dry. Serve hot garnished with sliced eggs and fried onions.

Methi pullao

250 grams rice. 2 bunches fenugreek leaves, cleaned and sliced. A pinch asafoetida. 4 tblsps. thick tamarind juice. 1 tblsp. each of coriander seeds, urad and channa dal. 1 tsp. cumin seeds. ½ tsp. turmeric powder. 4 red chillies. 1 tsp. sesame seeds. ½ cup grated dry coconut. Salt and jaggery to suit the taste.

Fry in a little oil coconut, dals, coriander, cumin and sesame seeds and asafoetida till red and grind to a paste. Boil the rice in the usual way. Dissolve jaggery in tamarind water. Heat 4 tblsps. oil and put in the methi and ground ingredients, turmeric and salt. Cover tightly and cook till the methi is done without adding water. Add tamarind and rice and mix well and cook over a slow fire till the rice turns dry. Serve hot.

Til rice

250 grams boiled rice. 2 tblsps. til or sesame seeds. 4 red chillies, broken into bits. A pinch of asafoetida. 1 tblsp. urad dal. 5 peppercorns. A few curry leaves. 1 tsp. lime juice. 50 grams fried cashewnuts.

Fry in a little ghee til, chillies, asafoetida, peppercorns and dal. When the dal turns red, remove and grind to a powder. Heat 1 tblsp. ghee and put in the curry leaves and salt, then rice and powdered ingredients and lime juice. Mix well and serve garnished with cashewnuts.

Tomato pullao

2 cups rice. 100 grams peeled and sliced tomatoes. 3 cups thin and 1 cup thick coconut milk. 4 cloves. 8 peppercorns. 2 cardamoms, peeled. ½-inch piece cinnamon stick, broken into bits. ½ tsp. turmeric powder. 1 onion, finely sliced. 25 grams fried cashewnuts. 2 hard-boiled eggs, shelled and quartered. Salt to taste.

Fry the onion till crisp and golden. Heat 2 tblsps. ghee and put in the whole spices and turmeric. Fry briefly then add tomatoes and salt and cook till the ghee floats to the top. Put in the rice. Mix well then pour in thin coconut milk, bring to a boil, reduce heat and cook till almost all the moisture is absorbed, then mix in boiling thick coconut milk, continue cooking till the rice is tender and dry, serve garnished with fried onions, cashewnuts and eggs.

Curd rice

250 grams boiled rice. Curds made from ½ litre milk. ½ cup milk. 25 grams minced ginger. A few curry leaves.

3 green chillies and 2 red chillies, minced. $\frac{1}{2}$ tsp. mustard seeds. Salt and chilli powder to taste.

Beat the curds nicely, put in milk and beat again till smooth. Mix in the rice. Heat 4 tblsps. ghee and put in mustard, when the seeds stop popping, put in the ginger, curry leaves, salt and chillies. When the ginger turns soft mix into the curd rice. Serve cold.

Hyderabadi moghlai biryani

250 grams Delhi rice. 750 grams boneless mutton preferably that of leg or shoulder. 1 big onion, finely sliced. 2 cups beaten curds. 1-inch piece ginger. 2 green and 2 red chillies. 2 small and 2 big cardamoms. 4 cloves. 1-inch piece cinnamon stick. A big pinch each of nutmeg and mace. 1 tsp. saffron strands. 4 tblsps. hot milk. 25 grams each of blanched and fried and sliced almonds, cashewnuts and raisins. Handful of seedless fresh grapes of various colours. 2 canned pineapple slices, cut into pieces. Silver foil. Salt to taste. A few drops each of orange, red and green food colouring. 2 tblsps. garam masala.

Grind ginger and chillies to a paste. Soak saffron in milk for 10 minutes then crush to a paste. Wash and wipe the mutton and cut into small pieces. Wash and soak the rice in 500 grams water for half an hour. Heat 1 cup ghee and put in the onions and fry till they turn limp. Add mutton after applying to it garam masala, ginger paste and salt and brown it nicely on all the sides. Put in the curds. Cover tightly and cook over a slow fire without adding water till the mutton turns tender and dry. Remove from fire and set aside. Heat 2 tblsps. ghee and put in the whole spices, then put in the rice along with the water in which it was soaked and salt. Bring to a boil, reduce heat and cook till the rice is almost tender and dry. Remove from fire and mix in saffron and divide into four equal portions. Colour one portion red, the second green, the third orange and leave one portion white. Then mix together the four different coloured rice. Take a large flame-proof greased glass dish. Place rice and mutton in layers in it, start and finish with a layer of rice. Cover tightly and cook over a very slow fire till the rice is completely tender and dry. Remove from fire, cover the surface with foil and arrange on top grapes and pineapple in any pattern you like. Serve piping hot.

Puli chorai

500 grams cooked rice. 150 grams tamarind. 100 grams til oil. 16 red chillies. 2 big onions, minced. 1 tblsp. coriander seeds. 2 tblsps. channa dal. 1 tblsp. urad dal. A pinch asafoetida. 25 grams each of fried cashewnuts and groundnuts. 1 tblsp. sesame seeds. A few curry leaves. ½ tsp. turmeric powder. 1 tsp. fenugreek seeds. 1 tblsp. mustard seeds. Salt to taste.

Fry fenugreek seeds, chillies, dals, til and coriander seeds and grind them to a paste. Cover tamarind with water for 5 minutes, then squeeze out thick juice. Heat oil and put in asafoetida and onions and turmeric powder and fry till the onions start changing colour. Add tamarind juice and cook till oil floats to the top. Mix in the rice and curry leaves with ground paste nicely and thoroughly and remove from fire. Serve hot garnished with nuts.

Ven pongal

250 grams rice. 1 cup moong dal. 1 tsp. peppercorns. 1 tsp. cumin seeds. 2-inch piece ginger, minced. 50 grams fried cashewnuts. 25 grams fried raisins. Salt to taste. A few curry leaves.

Heat 6 tblsps. ghee and add peppercorns and cumin seeds. When the seeds stop popping, add the dal and fry lightly, put in rice and salt and curry leaves and ginger along with enough water to stand 1-inch above the level of the rice. Bring the water to a boil, reduce heat to simmering and cook till the rice is completely tender and dry. Serve hot garnished with nuts and raisins.

Mussel pullao

3 cups Delhi rice. 100 big mussels. ½ cup thick coconut milk. 200 grams fried cashewnuts. 5 red chillies. 10 per-percorns. 5 flakes garlic. 1-inch piece ginger. 5 cloves. 2-

inch piece cinnamon stick. 1 tsp. turmeric powder. 4 cardamoms. Salt to suit the taste. 1 small piece coconut, cut into pieces and fried. Handful of coriander leaves.

Wash, clean and steam the mussels in their shells for 15 minutes, open lid and sprinkle cold water over them and steam them for 5 more minutes. The shells will open. Pick out mussels from shells and clean and wash them taking care not to break them. Grind chillies with all the spices and apply on the mussels and set aside for 15 minutes. Boil the rice in water along with salt and turmeric. When the rice is half boiled, drain out the water nicely and set aside. Fry the sliced onions till brown. Heat 6 tblsps. ghee and fry the mussels to a light brown colour and mix in cashewnuts and onions and remove from fire. Reserve a few cashewnuts for garnishing the pullao. Grease a flame-proof glass dish nicely and arrange alternate layers of rice and mussel mixture in it. Start and finish with a layer of rice. Put the coconut milk over the rice and dots of ghee here and there and cover tightly. Place over a very gentle flame and cook till the rice is tender. Serve in the dish itself garnished with remaining cashewnuts, fried coconut and coriander leaves.

Arvaha (Kerala)

2 cups rice. 750 grams finely grated jaggery. ½ cup ghee. 1 tsp. cardamom powder. 50 grams each of fried cashewnuts and raisins. 2-inch piece diced and fried coconut. A big pinch salt.

Cook the rice in 4 cups water. When the rice is cooked add jaggery and cardamom powder and continue cooking till the jaggery has melted. Add little ghee at a time stirring continuously. Remove from fire and serve decorated with coconut, raisins and cashewnuts.

SWEETS AND DESSERTS

Badami halwa

1 kilo wheat. 3 $\frac{1}{2}$ cups milk. 250 grams ghee. 1$\frac{1}{2}$ kilo sugar. 250 grams blanched and ground almonds. 50 grams blanched and sliced almonds. 1 tsp. saffron strands. 1 tsp. powdered cardamoms. $\frac{1}{4}$ tsp. grated nutmeg.

Clean the wheat and soak in water for 3 days changing the water daily. Soak saffron in 2 tblsps. hot milk for 10 minutes then grind or crush to a paste. Drain out the water from wheat and grind to a smooth and fine paste without adding water. Strain the wheat paste in a muslin cloth. Then add a little hot water to the residue and squeeze nicely. Throw away the barn left on the cloth after removing the milk. Keep the milk aside for 12 hours, then without disturbing the collected milk at the bottom throw away the thin water from the top. Place the wheat milk in a cloth and tie it up in a bundle and hang it up until all the water drains off. Place the milk and sugar in a heavy-bottomed vessel and make a thick syrup, put in the wheat lump and keep on stirring over a low fire till it turns thick, put in ground almonds and little ghee at a time, when all the ghee is used up and it starts leaving the halwa put in cardamoms, nutmeg and saffron, mix nicely and remove from fire. Put the halwa in a greased thali and garnish with sliced almonds. Set aside to turn cold, then cut into any shape you like with a sharp knife. Store in airtight container. Lasts for 1 week.

Wheat halwa

250 grams wheat flour. 500 grams jaggery. $\frac{1}{2}$ litre coconut milk. 1 tblsp. powdered cardamoms. $\frac{1}{4}$ tsp. grated nutmeg. 150 grams cashewnuts, sliced finely. 250 grams ghee.

Put enough water in flour to make a very soft dough. Set aside whole night, then pass through a fine sieve. Dissolve jaggery in 2 litres water them strain. Mix together

dough, jaggery syrup and coconut milk and cook over a
slow fire till the mixture turns thick, put in the cashewnuts, cardamoms and nutmeg. Mix well then put little
ghee at a time. When all the ghee has been used up and
it starts leaving the halwa, remove from fire and put in
a greased thali. Level the surface, cover with foil and
when cold cut into small pieces.

Pal cashewnut cake

2 litres milk. 250 grams ground cashewnuts. 250 grams
sugar. 1 tsp. essence of rose. 50 grams ghee. Silver foil.

Place milk and sugar together on fire. When the milk
turns thick, put in the cashewnuts and cook till the mixture turns very thick and leaves the sides of the vessel.
Then start putting a little ghee at a time, till all the ghee
is used up and absorbed by the cake. Now put in the
essence and remove from fire. Put the mixture in a greased
thali. Level the surface, cover with foil and cut into any
shape you like after it turns cold. Store in airtight container.

Rava pal cake

1 cup semolina or rava. 1 cup ghee. 1 cup finely grated
coconut. 1 cup milk. 2 cups sugar. 1 tsp. cardamom
powder. ¼ tsp. saffron strands. 25 grams finely chopped
cashewnuts. Silver foil.

Soak saffron in 1 tblsp. hot milk for 5 minutes, then
crush it to a paste. Put the rest of the above ingredients
in a heavy-bottomed vessel. Keep on stirring till the
mixture turns thick and starts leaving the sides of the
vessel. Stir in essence and remove from fire. Put in a
greased thali, cover with foil, cool and cut into any shape
you like. Store in airtight container.

Coconut cake

1 large coconut, grated finely. Sugar equal to the weight
of coconut. 1 tsp. coarsely ground cardamom powder.

A few drops yellow food colouring. 2 tblsps. ghee. A few finely sliced pistachio nuts. ½ tsp. essence of rose. Put coconut, sugar, cardamoms and ghee together in a pan and cook over a slow fire stirring all the time till the mixture turns thick and starts leaving the sides of the pan. Add essence, mix well and remove from fire and put half of it in a greased thali. Add colour to the remaining coconut and spread over the first layer. Sprinkle pistachios over the top. Cool and then cut into neat little squares with a sharp knife. Store in airtight container.

Sweet potato jamun

250 grams boiled and peeled sweet potatoes. 2 tblsps. refined flour or maida. 2 tblsps. cream. 1 tsp. coarsely pounded cardamoms. 25 grams blanched and ground almonds. 4 tblsps. finely grated coconut. 2 cups sugar. 1 tsp. essence of rose. Silver foil.

Mix together potatoes, cream and flour and knead to a smooth mixture. Also mix together cardamoms, almonds and coconut. Divide the potato and coconut mixture into equal number of portions. Form the potato mixture into balls around the coconut mixture. Deep fry over a slow fire to a golden colour. Drain, cover with foil and set aside. Add 1 cup water to sugar and prepare a syrup of one-thread consistency. Remove from fire, put in the jamuns, sprinkle essence on top and set aside for 5 minutes before serving them.

Dhamrotu

2 cups finely grated petah or red pumpkin. 25 grams each of raisins and almonds. A few cashewnuts, halved. ¼ tsp. essence of saffron. 2 cups fine semoline or suji. 1 tsp. cardamom powder. 2 cups sugar. A big pinch nutmeg.

Cook the vegetable in its own juice till soft. Fry almonds and raisins and slice finely. Boil 1½ cups water and put in suji after frying it to a red colour in ¼ cup ghee.

Cover for 3 minutes then put in sugar and keep on stirring till the sugar is dissolved. Add pumpkin, almonds, spices, raisins and essence and keep on stirring till the mixture leaves the sides of the vessel, remove from fire and put in a greased thali, level the surface and set aside to turn cold, cut into any shape you like and decorate the top with a halved cashewnut. Shallow fry over a slow fire till they turn brown and crisp. Drain and serve hot.

Chimmili (Andhra Pradesh)

500 grams each of sesame seeds and finely grated jaggery. 25 grams each of sliced raisins, roasted peanuts and pistachios and roasted grams. 1 tsp. coarsely pounded cardamom seeds. 2 tblsps. ghee.

Roast til on a dry girdle till the seeds turn light golden in colour. Pound peanuts and pistachios coarsely. Put jaggery and ghee together on fire, when the jaggery turns into a syrup, put in the rest of the above ingredients and remove from fire. Cool till bearably hot, then quickly form into round balls, set aside to turn cold then store in airtight tin.

Peanut ladu

500 grams each of roasted peanuts and finely grated jaggery. 1 tsp. coarsely pounded cardamom seeds. 2 tblsps. ghee.

Pound the nuts coarsely. Melt ghee, add jaggery and prepare a syrup, put in the remaining ingredients, mix well and remove from fire. Dust your hands with rice flour and prepare round balls. Set aside to turn cold and then store in airtight tin.

Boondi ladu

250 grams gram flour. Pinch of baking powder. A few drops of orange red food colouring. 1 tblsp. cardamom seeds. 50 grams fried and diced cashewnuts. 4 tblsps. milk. 25 grams each of sugar candy and raisins. 4 cloves. $\frac{1}{4}$ tsp. grated nutmeg. 1 tblsp. rice flour. 250 grams sugar.

Mix together flour, baking powder, milk, colour and then add enough water to form a thick batter. Coarsely pound cloves and sugar candy. Blend together sugar, and 1 cup water and form a syrup of one-thread consistency. Remove from fire and keep it warm. Beat the batter till it turns very smooth and free of all lumps. Heat enough ghee for deep frying to smoking, lower heat then take a sieve, hold it over the smoking ghee and rub a little batter at a time through the sieve. Tap the sieve on the inside edges of the pan to make the mixture fall through the holes into the ghee. Fry the boondi to a golden colour. Drain thoroughly and put into syrup. In this way as soon as one batch of boondi is done put it into the syrup. When all the mixture is used up and the boondi is in the syrup, put in the rest of the above ingredients. Mix thoroughly. If the mixture is a little dry sprinkle a little hot milk over it. Put 2 tblsps. of hot melted ghee over the mixture and mix again thoroughly. Grease your hands and shape into round balls. Set aside to turn hard then store in airtight tin.

Podivilengai ladu

500 grams moong dal. 500 grams grated jaggery. 1 tblsp. cardamom seeds. 75 grams wheat. ¼ dry coconut, finely sliced.

Roast dal and wheat to a red colour then powder them. Put 2 cups water in jaggery. When it dissolves, put in cardamoms and coconut and cook till the syrup strings a thread. Put in the powdered dal. Mix thoroughly and remove from fire. Dust your hands with rice flour and go on making ladus quickly from the hot mixture. When the ladus turn dry and hard store in airtight container. If you will allow the mixture even to cool a little you will not be able to form ladus as it will then turn very hard like toffee.

Jhangiri

500 grams urad dal. 75 grams rice. A few drops orange red food colouring. 750 grams sugar. 1 tsp. essence of rose.

Put 1 glass of water in sugar and prepare a syrup of one-thread consistency. Add essence, remove from fire and keep it warm. Soak dal and rice whole night separately in water. Next morning, drain out the water and grind both of them together to a very smooth paste. Put in colour and little milk to make a thick batter. Heat enough ghee for deep frying to smoking, lower the heat, then pour the batter into a thick cloth bag with a hole and form two rounds together in the ghee, the one round should be around the other. Then form small scallops or rounds all round the two big rounds. Deep fry each jhangiri to a golden colour. Drain nicely and toss into the syrup. After 10 minutes, remove from the syrup and arrange on a clean plate. You can keep them for a fortnight.

Modak

500 grams rice flour. 1 coconut, finely grated. 250 grams finely grated jaggery. 7 cardamoms, peeled.

Place coconut, jaggery and cardamoms on a slow fire and cook till thick. Boil 375 grams of water add the flour gradually stirring all the time. Cook on a slow fire till the flour turns dry and thick like dough. Remove from fire, rub a tablespoon of oil on it and knead to a very smooth dough. Divide the dough and the coconut mixture into equal number of portions. Form each portion of dough into a cup, stuff with coconut mixture and form the cup in the shape of a pyramid. Steam for half an hour and serve either hot or cold.

Koykotay

250 grams rice flour. 125 grams sugar, powdered. Thick coconut milk. 1 tsp. ground cardamoms.

Mix flour, sugar and cardamoms. Put in enough coconut milk to form a stiff dough. Divide into small pieces, shape each piece into a ball and steam for half an hour.

Rose Cruickeese (Kerala)

2 cups refined flour or maida. 1 egg, lightly beaten. 1 cup milk. 3 tblsps. sugar. ½ tblsp. essence of rose.

Mix all the above ingredients together and beat till the batter turns very smooth. Heat enough ghee for deep frying to smoking, take a mould shaped like a rose and dip it in the hot ghee till it is heated nicely, then remove and dip the mould in the batter just enough to get a coating of the batter round the sides and the bottom of the mould. Transfer the mould back into the hot ghee. After a few seconds rose-shaped cruickeese or cookies will slip out into the ghee. Lift out the mould from the ghee and deep fry the cookies till crisp and light golden coloured. Drain nicely, cool and store in airtight container.

Kalkals (Kerala)

500 grams rice flour. 75 grams urad dal. 1 tsp. cardamom powder. 75 grams sugar.

Wash and soak dal in water for 5 hours. Drain and grind to a smooth paste. Mix with flour and enough coconut milk to make a soft and pliable dough. Put 3 cups of water in sugar and prepare a syrup of one-thread consistency. Put in cardamoms, remove from fire and keep it warm. Now take small pieces of dough and flatten out on a fork, then roll each piece off so that the design of the fork will be imprinted on it. Deep fry till crisp and golden, drain and put into the syrup, when the syrup starts to dry, mix them thoroughly, then separate each kalkal and place on a clean plate to turn dry and hard. Store in airtight containers.

Samosi

250 grams refined flour or maida. A pinch soda bicarb. A big pinch salt. 1 tblsp. ghee.

For filling . . . . 250 grams channa dal. 250 grams powdered sugar. 50 grams fried cashewnuts. 25 grams poppy seeds. ¼ dry coconut. 1 tsp. powdered cardamoms. Roast dal till light golden. Also roast poppy seeds. Pound together to a powder dal, poppy seeds, cashewnuts. Mix in sugar and finely sliced dry copra and cardamoms. Mix together flour, salt and soda. Rub in fat, then add enough water to form a stiff dough. Knead well. Divide the dough and the stuffing into equal number of portions. Roll out each piece of dough into a round disc, put the stuffing evenly on one side of the disc, fold over to form crescents, then seal the edges. Decorate edges and deep fry till light golden. Drain nicely, cool and store in airtight containers.

Dal holige (Mysore)

250 grams fine semolina. 125 grams refined flour or maida. Pinch each of baking powder and salt. A big pinch turmeric powder. 4 tblsps. gingelly oil.

For filling . . . . 125 grams channa dal. ½ coconut, finely grated. 200 grams finely grated jaggery. 1 tsp. cardamom powder.

Blend together flour with all the dry ingredients and pass through a sieve. Rub in oil, then add enough water to form a soft and pliable dough. Wash and soak dal in water for 2 hours, then cook in water in which it was soaked till tender and completely dry. Remove from fire and grind to a paste with coconut and jaggery. Put back upon heat and cook on slow fire till the mixture thickens and it gives out a pleasant smell. Mix in the cardamom powder and remove from fire. Divide the dough and the filling into equal number of portions. Roll out each portion of dough as thinly as you can with the help of a little dry flour, place the filling in the centre and gather the edges together over the filling. Press gently on a greased banana leaf or the back of a stainless steel thali then shallow fry on a girdle to a golden brown colour. Serve hot with pure ghee and milk.

Mandige holige (Mysore)

250 grams fine semolina. 125 grams refined flour or maida. Pinch each of baking powder and salt. A big pinch turmeric powder. 4 tblsps. gingelly oil.

For filling . . . . 200 grams poppy seeds. ½ tsp. saffron strands. 1 tsp. cardamom powder. 200 grams ground sugar. 2 tsps. ghee.

Pound all the filling ingredients to a fine powder. Put in ghee and pound again to a fine and smooth dough. Mix together semolina, flour, baking powder, salt and turmeric. Pass through a sieve, rub in oil then add enough water to form a soft and pliable dough. Divide the dough and the filling into equal number of portions. Now follow the procedure for making holiges as shown in the above recipe.

Sweet potato holige (Mysore)

1 cup flour. A pinch each of baking powder and salt. 1 tblsp. gingelly oil. A big pinch turmeric powder.

For filling . . . . 250 grams sweet potatoes, boiled and peeled. ½ cup finely grated jaggery. 1 tsp. cardamom powder.

Mix together flour, salt, turmeric and baking powder. Rub in oil, then add enough water to form a soft and pliable dough. Grind sweet potatoes and jaggery to a paste and mix in the cardamoms. Divide the dough and filling into equal number of portions and make holiges shown in the recipe entitled Dal Holige.

Appam (Mysore)

100 grams rice. 75 grams finely grated jaggery. Milk. ¼ finely grated coconut. ½ tsp. pepper.

Wash and soak rice for a few hours. Drain and grind to a paste. Mix in jaggery and grind once again till smooth and thick. Pour in enough milk to form a thick batter. Mix in pepper and coconut and drop teaspoonfuls of batter in hot ghee, deep fry to a golden brown colour. Drain thoroughly and serve hot.

Rus vade

500 grams rice. 25 grams grated jaggery. 1 coconut. Salt to taste.

Extract milk from coconut. Wash and dry rice then powder it. Mix together flour, jaggery and salt and put in enough coconut milk to form a soft and pliable dough. Divide the dough into lime-sized portions. **Press each piece of dough with your hand on a greased banana leaf to ½-inch thick vada and deep fry in oil till golden brown coloured. Drain thoroughly before serving.**

Plantain muluks

200 grams ripe bananas. 100 grams semolina. 30 grams coconut, finely grated. 50 grams finely grated jaggery. Salt to taste.

Peel and mash the bananas to a paste. Mix in the rest of the above ingredients and form a soft and sticky dough. Form the dough into small balls and deep fry to a golden brown colour. Drain and serve hot or cold.

Egg halwa (Mysore)

2 eggs. 1 tblsp. roasted channa dal. 5 cashewnuts, fried. 5 fried almonds. 1 tblsp. finely sliced dry coconut. 25 fried raisins. 1 tsp. cardamom powder. 3 tblsps. sugar. 10 groundnuts, roasted.

Fry coconut and pound coarsely, also pound the nuts, dal and sugar. Beat eggs nicely and mix in the coconut and pounded ingredients and cardamom powder. Heat 2 tblsps. ghee and put in the egg mixture. Keep on stirring over a slow fire till the egg sets. Mix nicely till smooth, remove from fire and garnish with raisins. Serve hot.

Pumpkin halwa (Mysore)

250 grams finely grated pumpkin. ½ litre milk. 1 tsp. cardamom powder. 1 tsp. poppy seeds. 25 grams fried cashewnuts and raisins. 100 grams sugar.

Place pumpkin and milk together in a pan and cook over a slow fire till the pumpkin turns tender and thick. Put in sugar, cardamoms and poppy seeds and keep on stirring till the halwa turns thick and dry. Remove from fire, mash to a paste and serve immediately garnished with cashewnuts and raisins. You can put in a few drops of green food colouring to give it a nice green colour.

Thali sweet

1½ cups semolina. ¾ cup finely grated jaggery. 1½ cup coconut milk. 3 ripe bananas. 2 tblsps. water. A pinch of salt. Handful of splitted almonds or cashewnuts. 1 tsp. cardamom powder.

Heat 2 tblsps. ghee and fry semolina to a golden brown colour. Peel and mash the bananas and mix with semolina and the rest of the above ingredients with the exception of almonds. Spread the mixture in a greased thali and decorate with split almonds. Steam for about 20 minutes, or until a toothpick inserted in the centre comes out clean. Cut into neat little cubes with a sharp knife and serve either hot or cold.

Banana puffs

2 cups sifted refined flour or maida. Pinch of salt. 2 tblsps. ghee. 3 ripe bananas, peeled and mashed. 4 tblsps. grated coconut. Buttermilk. Pinch of baking powder.

Blend together flour, salt and baking powder. Rub in ghee then add enough buttermilk or water to form a stiff dough. Roll out the dough into a big round disc, and cut into small rounds with the help of a biscuit cutter or an inverted glass. Add coconut to bananas and mix nicely. Place a teaspoon of banana mixture on one side of the round, fold over like crescents and seal the edges. Deep fry to a golden colour. Drain thoroughly and serve either hot or cold.

Sato

1 cup flour. ¼ cup each of ghee, rice and gram flour. 2 cups sugar. Seeds of large cardamoms.

Blend together all the flours with ghee and ¼ cup water to form a dough. Knead well, then form the dough into round cherries. Press a couple of cardamom seeds on either side of the cherry and deep fry to a golden colour. Drain and set aside. Mix 2 cups of sugar and 1 cup of water and prepare a syrup of one-thread consistency.

Put in the fried cherries and mix thoroughly then set aside till the syrup begins to dry. Remove the cherries from the syrup one by one and keep aside to turn dry completely. Store in airtight containers. Sato is mostly served at weddings.

Seviyan (Hyderabad)

2 cups slightly broken vermecelli. 1 cup sugar. Handful each of fried and sliced almonds and pistachios. 25 grams each of fried raisins, charoli and cashewnuts. 1 tsp. coarsely powdered cardamom seeds. 1 tsp. essence of rose. Silver foil.

Mix together sugar with 2 cups water over a slow fire, when the sugar dissolves into the water remove from fire. Heat 3 tblsps. ghee and fry the vermecelli to a golden brown colour. Pour in the sugar syrup and cook over a slow fire till the vermecelli is tender and completely dry. When ready the vermecelli must be a beautiful golden colour and each vermecelli strand should be separate, not mushy or sticking together. Mix in the nuts and rose water and remove from fire. Serve hot or cold decorated with foil.

Khiri (Mangalore)

1 cup rice. ¼ coconut, ground finely. 1 cup finely grated jaggery. 1½ cups thick coconut milk. 1 tsp. cardamom powder.

Wash and soak rice in water for 4 hours. Drain and grind to a paste. Mix in coconut, form into small round cherries and deep fry to a golden colour. Drain and set aside. Mix 2 cups water in jaggery and prepare quite a thick syrup. Put in the cherries and boil for 5 minutes. Pour in coconut milk and bring slowly to a boil. Remove from fire and sprinkle cardamom powder on top.

Semiya payasam

100 grams vermecelli. 1 litre milk. 1½ cups sugar. 50 grams fried cashewnuts. 25 grams fried raisins. 1 tsp. cardamom powder.

Heat 2 tblsps. ghee and fry vermecelli to a golden brown colour. Add milk. Cook till the vermecelli turns soft and the mixture quite thick. Put in the sugar and keep on stirring till the sugar dissolves. Remove from fire and serve hot garnished with cashewnuts, raisins and cardamom powder.

Rice payasam

1 cup broken rice. ¾ cup grated jaggery. 2½ cups thin coconut milk and 1 cup thick coconut milk. 1 tsp. ground cardamoms. 25 grams fried cashewnuts.

Cook rice in thin coconut milk till it turns soft. Add jaggery and cook till the jaggery is dissolved. Pour in thick coconut milk, bring slowly to a boil, remove from fire and serve hot garnished with cashewnuts and powdered cardamoms.

Kadale bele payasa (Mysore)

2 cups coconut milk. 2 cups milk. 2½ cups finely grated jaggery. ¾ cup channa dal. 50 grams fried cashewnuts. 1 tsp. ground cardamoms. 2 tblsps. finely sliced coconut, fried.

Boil dal till very soft in little water. Remove and grind to a paste. Add milk and coconut milk and cook till thick. Put in the jaggery and keep on stirring till the jaggery is dissolved. Serve hot garnished with cashewnuts, coconut and cardamom powder.

Arsi payasam

1 cup broken rice. ½ cup moong dal. 2½ cups grated jaggery. 2 cups coconut milk. 25 grams each of fried cashewnuts and raisins. 1 tsp. cardamom powder.

Fry both rice and dal in little ghee till they turn light golden coloured, then pour in 4 cups water and cook till soft. Add jaggery and cardamom powder and stir till the jaggery is dissolved. Pour in coconut milk and keep on stirring till the payasam turns quite thick. Serve garnished with cashewnuts and raisins.

Banana payasam (Kerala)

250 grams finely grated jaggery. 6 ripe bananas, peeled and sliced. Thin and thick milk of 1 big coconut. $\frac{1}{4}$ coconut, finely sliced. 1 tsp. cardamom powder. 25 grams raisins.

Fry the raisins and sliced coconut to a red colour in ghee. Pour 2 cups of water in jaggery and prepare a syrup. Remove from fire. Put little water in bananas and cook till soft. Mash them well, add syrup, bring to a boil, then add thin milk and cook till thick. Pour in thick milk and cardamom powder. When the payasam reaches simmering point, remove and serve decorated with coconut and raisins.

Pumpkin payasam (Kerala)

2 cups pumpkin or marrow, boiled and mashed. Thin and thick milk of 1 big coconut. 500 grams grated jaggery. 2 tblsps. honey. 25 grams fried raisins. 25 grams fried cashewnuts. 1 tsp. cardamom powder.

Put 1 glass water in jaggery and prepare a syrup. Mix honey and 2 tblsps. ghee in pumpkin and bring to a boiling point, reduce heat and put in the thin milk and syrup and cook till thick. Add thick milk and cardamom powder and heat to simmering. Serve decorated with fried raisins and cashewnuts.

Mango payasam (Kerala)

3 ripe mangoes. 1 cup finely grated jaggery. 1 cup thick milk of coconut. 1 tsp. cardamom powder. 4 tblsps. ghee.

Put 2 cups water in jaggery and prepare a syrup. Peel and slice the mangoes. Cook the mangoes in little water till soft, add syrup and cook till thick. Add ghee a little at a time till all is used up. Put in coconut milk, heat to simmering and remove from fire, sprinkle cardamom powder on top before serving.

Dal payasam (Mangalore)

¾ cup moong dal. 2 cups finely grated jaggery. 2 cups thin and 1 cup thick coconut milk. 1 tsp. powdered cardamoms. Ghee. 25 grams each of fried raisins and cashewnuts.

Roast dal to a red colour then pour into it thin milk and cook till the dal turns soft. Add jaggery and keep on stirring till the mixture turns thick. Add thick coconut milk and cook on a slow fire till the payasam turns thick like custard. Remove from fire, sprinkle nuts and cardamom powder on top. Serve in individual plates and top each plate with a tablespoon of pure ghee.

Ghee payasam (Kerala)

½ cup rice. 400 grams finely grated jaggery. ¼ cup ghee. 50 grams sugar candy broken into tiny bits. ¼ cup honey. 50 grams fried raisins. 25 grams each of fried cashewnuts and almonds. 1 tsp. cardamom powder.

Cook rice in 1 cup water, when it turns soft add jaggery and cook till the jaggery is absorbed into the rice. Put in ghee, cardamom powder, sugar candy and honey. Mix thoroughly and remove from fire. Serve hot decorated with nuts and raisins.

Ada payasam (Kerala)

1 cup rice. Thin and thick milk of 2 coconuts. 400 grams finely grated jaggery. 1 tsp. cardamom powder. 25 grams each of fried raisins and cashewnuts. Pinch of salt.

Soak rice in water for a couple of hours, drain out the water and pound finely, add salt and 4 tblsps. ghee and enough hot water to form a thin batter. Spread the batter on a clean plantain leaf, roll up the leaf, tie with a thread and steam for half an hour. Cool and cut the adas into small pieces. Put 1 glass water in jaggery, when the jaggery melts, strain through a cloth and prepare a syrup of one-thread consistency, put in 2 tblsps. ghee and prepared adas and cook till the mixture turns thin, put in thin milk and continue cooking till the mixture turns thick once again, pour in thick milk, bring to simmering point and remove from fire. Serve hot decorated with raisins, cashewnuts and cardamom powder.

Apricot pudding (Hyderabad)

4 cups milk, boiled. 3 eggs, beaten. A pinch of salt. 6 tblsps. sugar. 1 tsp. vanilla essence. 125 grams dry apricots. Handful of mixed sliced nuts.

Wash and boil apricots in a little water till soft. Remove from fire, stone and mash to a paste. Combine together sugar, eggs and salt, pour in the milk and place on top of simmering water. Cook the mixture stirring all the time till it coats the spoon. Remove from fire and mix in the apricots and essence. Chill nicely and serve garnished with nuts.

Sweet potato pudding

2 cups ground fresh coconut. 2 cups milk. 4 sweet potatoes, boiled, peeled and mashed. 4 tblsps. finely grated coconut. A few drops of vanilla essence. Sugar to taste. Put ground coconut and milk together in a pan, bring to a boil, remove from fire and cool nicely then press out the liquid from the coconut. Mix together sweet potatoes, powdered sugar and coconut milk and essence and beat with an egg beater till light and fluffy. Pour the mixture in a shallow greased baking dish and bake in a moderate oven for 15 to 20 minutes or till a toothpick inserted in the centre comes out clean. Fry the grated coconut to a golden colour and sprinkle over the pudding before serving.

Sago halwa

1 cup sago. 3 cups milk. ½ cup ghee. ¼ tsp. saffron. 25 grams each of fried cashewnuts and raisins. 1 tblsp. cardamom powder. 2 cups sugar.

Mix 1 cup water in sugar and prepare a syrup of one-thread consistency. Remove from fire and keep it warm. Soak saffron in 1 tsp. hot milk for 5 minutes, then grind to a paste. Heat 2 tblsps. ghee and fry the sago to a golden colour. Remove from fire and set aside. Boil the milk, add sago and cook till the mixture turns thick. Put in the syrup add cardamoms and cook over a slow fire till the halwa turns thick and leaves the sides of the vessel. Mix in the saffron add raisins and remove from fire. Put the halwa in a greased thali and level the surface. Garnish with cashewnuts and cut into squares when cold and set. Store in airtight containers. Lasts for a couple of days.

Sago poli

1 cup sago. 1 cup of maida. ½ cup grated coconut. ¼ tsp. saffron. 1 tsp. cardamom powder, 2 cups sugar. 10 fried cashewnuts. 10 fried raisins. A pinch of salt. A pinch turmeric powder.

Mix together salt, turmeric and flour. Rub in 1 tblsp. oil and then add enough water to make a soft and pliable dough. Put ½ cup water in sugar and prepare a syrup of one-thread consistency. Remove from fire and keep it warm. Soak sago in 2 cups water for one hour, then boil it in the water in which it was soaked till soft and completely dry. Remove from fire and grind it to a paste along with coconut. Soak saffron in 1 tsp. hot milk for 5 minutes, then grind to a paste. Slice the cashewnuts and raisins. Mix together sago, sugar syrup, saffron, nuts and raisins and cook over a slow fire till the mixture turns thick and leaves the sides of the vessel. Divide the dough and the sago mixture into equal number of portions. Roll out each portion of dough into a round disc, place a portion of sago in the middle of the disc and gather the edges together. Press gently on a greased banana leaf or a back of a greased thali into a thick puri or disc and shallow fry to a golden colour. Serve piping hot.

Neyyappam

1½ cups rice flour. ½ cup maida. 1 tsp. baking powder. 1 small banana, mashed finely. 150 grams grated jaggery. 1 tsp. ground cardamom seeds. 1 small piece finely grated coconut.

Melt jaggery in half cup water over low fire, then strain. Remove cool and mix in the remaining ingredients and form a thick batter. Add more water if the batter is not of the required consistency. Drop teaspoonfuls of batter in smoking ghee and deep fry to a golden brown colour. Drain and serve piping hot.

Munthri kothu

1 kilo green gram. 300 grams finely grated jaggery. 1 coconut, finely grated. 1 tsp. cardamom powder. 100 grams til seeds. 200 grams rice. 1 tblsp. urad dal.

Soak rice and dal whole night in water. Next morning, drain and grind to a smooth paste. Add enough hot water to make into a thick batter. Roast gram till light golden and it gives out a fine aroma. Powder finely. Roast coconut and til to a nice brown colour. Put 1 cup water in jaggery and prepare a syrup of one-thread consistency. Put in gram powder, til, coconut and cardamoms and mix till the mixture leaves the sides of the vessel, remove from heat, cool till bearably hot, form into small balls. Put 2 or 3 balls together so that when frying they stick together giving the appearance of a bunch of grapes. Deep fry to a golden brown colour.

Ukkarai

200 grams green gram dal. 200 grams gram dal. 500 grams finely grated jaggery. 200 grams ghee. A big pinch

salt. ½ finely grated coconut. 1 tsp. coarsely pounded cardamom seeds. ¼ tsp. essence of saffron. 100 grams cashewnuts, fried and coarsely chopped. Silver or golden foil.

Soak the dals in water for a couple of hours, drain and grind to a thick paste. Roast the coconut to a nice golden colour. Heat half of the ghee and fry the dal paste to a nice golden colour. Put 1 cup water in jaggery and prepare a syrup of one-thread consistency. Put in all the above ingredients with the exception of essence and keep on stirring till the mixture leaves the sides of the vessel. Remove from fire and put in a greased plate. Mix in the essence and level the surface, cover with foil and set aside to turn cold. Cut into pieces and store in airtight tins.

Mysore Pak

250 grams besan or gram flour. 250 grams sugar. 500 grams ghee. 1 tsp. cardamom powder. ¼ tsp. essence of safiron. 25 grams sliced pistachios and almonds. Silver or golden foil.

Put 1 cup water in sugar and prepare a syrup of one-thread consistency. Fry gram flour in 100 grams ghee to a nice golden colour. Add the nuts, sugar syrup, cardamoms and a few drops of yellow food colouring, and mix well Heat remaining ghee to smoking and put the ghee gradually into the pak stirring all the time. When the mixture is well-bended and the ghee begins to appear on the surface, mix in the essence, remove from fire and put in a greased thali. Cover with foil and cut into squares while still warm and leave to set till hard.

Ghee balls

500 grams gram dal. 250 grams rice. 500 grams sugar. Hot ghee. 25 grams fried and sliced raisins. 1 tsp. cardamom powder. 50 grams fried and finely sliced cashewnuts.

Roast the dal to a nice red colour and powder. Powder the rice. Also powder sugar. Mix together all the above ingredients with the exception of ghee, then add enough ghee to hold the ingredients together. Mix nicely and shape into big balls while still hot.

Dal obbattu (Mysore)

250 grams toovar dal. 500 grams finely grated jaggery. 1 tblsp. charoli. 1 tblsp. raisins. 25 grams each of almonds and pistachios. 1 tsp. cardamom powder. A few drops essence of saffron. 1½ cups coconut, grated finely. 250 grams maida. 100 grams flour.

Wash and cook the dal with very little water till tender. Mix together both the flours, rub in 2 tblsps. ghee and then add enough water to make a dough of medium consistency. Grind the dal to a paste along with coconut and jaggery without adding water. Stir the mixture on a slow fire till it turns thick. Remove from fire and mix in the nuts, cardamoms and essence. Divide the dough and the filling into equal number of portions. Make a small round disc from each portion of dough, put dal in the centre and cover it up. Press into a round shape again on a greased banana leaf or a thali. Shallow fry to a nice golden colour. Serve hot.

Bobbatlu (Andhra Pradesh)

500 grams gram dal. 1 tblsp. each of sliced raisins. 25 grams each of finely sliced almonds and pistachios. 500 grams ground sugar. A few drops essence of saffron. Milk. Pinch of salt. 500 grams maida.

Cook dal with very little water till soft. Grind to a paste without adding water and mix in the nuts, essence and sugar. Mix together flour and salt, add enough milk to form a soft dough. Divide the dough and the dal mixture into equal number of portions. Now follow the remaining procedure of tne above recipe to prepare Bobbatlu.

Panchakadai

1 big coconut, finely grated. 1 teacup each of gram dal and fine beaten rice. 200 grams finely grated jaggery. 1 tsp. cardamom powder.

Wash the dal and soak it in little water for a few hours, drain and grind in coarsely. Fry in ¼ cup ghee to a nice golden brown colour. Also fry the coconut and beaten rice. Pound the rice coarsely. Put ½ cup water in jaggery and prepare a syrup of one-thread consistency, put in the rest of the above ingredients and mix till the mixture starts leaving the sides of the vessel. Put in a greased thali, level the surface, set aside to turn cold, then cut into pieces.

Wheat flour halwa no. 1

500 grams flour. 1 kilo sugar. 1 litre milk. 1½ litres water. 500 grams melted smoking ghee. 250 grams chopped cashewnuts. 1 tblsp. coarsely pounded cardamom seeds. ¼ tsp. essence of saffron. 2 tblsps. poppy seeds. 25 grams sliced almonds and pistachios.

Put enough water in flour to prepare a thick batter. Cover and set aside whole night. Next morning, pass through a muslin cloth. Put wheat batter, sugar, milk and water together in a heavy-bottomed vessel and cook till thick. Add essence, cardamoms and all the nuts with the exception of pistachios. Add ghee and keep on stirring till a small portion rolled between the thumb and the forefinger will form a non-sticky ball. Remove from fire and put in a greased thali, level the surface, decorate with pistachios and leave to cool, then cut into small pieces.

Wheat flour halwa no. 2

500 grams flour. 1 kilo grated jaggery. 1 litre coconut milk. 1½ litres water. 500 grams melted ghee. 250 grams chopped cashewnuts. 1 tblsp. cardamom powder. Silver foil.

S. I. C.—7

Put enough water in flour to prepare a thick batter. Cover and set aside whole night. Next morning, pass through a muslin cloth. Put wheat batter, jaggery after dissolving it over given quantity of water and coconut milk together in a heavy-bottomed vessel and cook till thick. Add cashewnuts, cardamoms and ghee and cook till a small portion of halwa rolled between the thumb and the forefinger forms a non-sticky ball. Put in a greased thali, level the surface, cover with foil and set aside to turn cold then cut into small pieces and store in airtight tins.

Rice flour halwa

500 grams rice flour. 350 grams finely grated jaggery. 1½ litres coconut milk. 1 tsp. cardamom powder. 50 grams chopped cashewnuts. A big pinch salt.

Mix together flour and milk and pass through a muslin to free of all lumps. Put into a vessel along with the rest of the above ingredients and cook till the mixture turns thick. Add 50 grams melted ghee and continue cooking til the mixture leaves the sides of the vessel. Put in a well-greased thali, level the surface, set aside to turn cold and cut into small pieces.

Sooji halwa

100 grams semolina or suji. 100 grams sugar. 50 grams ghee. 1 tsp. cardamom powder. 2 cups milk. A few drops yellow food colouring. 25 grams each of fried cashewnuts and raisins. 2 rings pineapple cubed.

Heat ghee and fry sooji to a light golden colour. Add milk, sugar and cardamoms and colour and cook till thick. Mix in the nuts and raisins and remove from fire. Serve decorated with pineapple.

Kompal

1 cup rice flour. 1½ cups sliced jackfruit. ½ cup grated jaggery. 1 cup grated coconut. 1 tsp. cardamom powder. A pinch of salt.

Grind coconut, jaggery and jackfruit to a paste. Mix with the rest of the above ingredients and form into balls. Steam for half an hour and serve atonce.

Jackfruit appam

2 cups flour. 1½ mups grated jaggery. 2 cups diced jackfruit. 1 cup grated coconut. 1 tsp. yeast. A big pinch salt.

Mash the fruit nicely and mix with the rest of the above ingredients. Add enough hot water to form a thin batter. Set aside for 1 hour. Fill greased katories half full with the mixture and steam till firm. Serve hot.

Kallapom (Kerala)

2 cups fine rice. 2 coconuts. ¼ cup toddy. ½ cup sugar.

Soak the rice whole night in water. Next morning, drain and grind the rice and coconut to a paste in coconut water. Add toddy and set aside for a few hours. Mix in the sugar. Put in a greased mould and steam till firm, when cold cut into pieces and serve.

MUTTON, CHICKEN AND PORK

500 grams mutton. 100 grams each of ghee and curds. 25 grams each of raisins, grapes and cashewnuts. ½ tsp. each of cumin and mustard seeds. 2 tsps. coriander seeds. 1 tsp. shahjeera. 3 cardamoms. 4 cloves. 1-inch piece cinnamon stick. 2-inch piece ginger. 4 red and 4 green chillies. Handful of sliced coriander leaves. Salt to taste.

Grind together all the spices, ginger and chillies to a paste. Mix the paste into the curds. Heat ghee and fry the mutton to a golden colour. Add curds a little at a time, when it dries up add more till all the curds is used up. Pour in ½ glass of hot water, salt, cashewnuts, raisins and grapes. Cover tightly and cook till the mutton is tender and almost dry. Serve garnished with coriander leaves.

Lukami (Hyderabad)

250 grams refined flour. 1 tsp. shahjeera. 1 tsp. pepper. 1 tblsp. ghee. Salt to taste.

For filling......250 grams minced mutton or kheema. 50 grams sliced onions. 3 cloves. 3 cardamoms. 1 bay leaf. ¼-inch piece cinnamon stick. 5 green chillies. 3 flakes garlic. 1-inch piece ginger. 1 tsp. each of coriander and cumin seeds. 2 red chillies. Salt to taste.

Grind all the spices to a paste with chillies, ginger and garlic. Put all the filling ingredients in a pan and cook over a slow fire without adding water till the mutton is completely tender. Remove from fire and set aside. Mix together flour, salt, pepper and shahjeera. Rub in ghee then add enough water to form a stiff dough. Roll out the dough as thinly as you can without breaking it with the help of a little dry flour. Cut the rolled out dough into neat squares. Place a tablespoon of filling over one square, cover with another square and seal the edges with

wet fingers. Deep fry to a golden brown colour. Drain
and serve hot with chutney of choice.

Lagan ka kabab (Hyderabad)

500 grams boneless mutton preferably of leg or shoulder,
cut into 1-inch pieces. 2-inch piece of ginger and raw
papaya. 6 flakes garlic. ½ cup ghee. 1 tblsp. garam masala.
1 tsp. pepper. Salt to taste.

Beat each piece of mutton with the handle of a knife
till flat. Grind ginger, garlic and papaya to a paste and
rub into the pieces of mutton along with salt. Set aside
for 1 hour. Heat ghee and fry the mutton to a red colour.
Cover tightly and sprinkle cold water on the lid. Cook
till the mutton is tender. If the water on the lid dries add
more water till the mutton is done.   Serve sprinkled
with garam masala and pepper.

Mutton chaps (Hyderabad)

8 big mutton chaps. 3 large potatoes, boiled and peeled.
Mint chutney......see chapter entitled Chutneys and
pickles. 4 flakes garlic. 2-inch piece ginger. 2 well-beaten
eggs. 1 cup fine bread crumbs. Salt to taste.

Grind ginger, salt and garlic to a paste and apply on the
chaps after flattening them with the handle of a knife.
The chaps should have long bones so that while eating
them you can hold the chaps by the bones. Steam-cook
the chaps. Mash the potatoes nicely. Add salt and knead
to a smooth mixture. Apply green chutney on both the
sides of the chaps. Then cover each chap nicely and
thoroughly with potato mixture leaving the bones. Roll
in crumbs, dip in beaten eggs and roll once again in
crumbs, then deep fry to a golden brown colour. Drain
and serve piping hot.

Kheema tikki (Hyderabad)

250 grams boiled and ground minced meat or kheema.
1 tsp. garam masala. 1 tblsp. each of grated coconut and
gram flour. ½-inch piece ginger, minced. 2 garlic flakes,

minced. 4 green chillies, minced. 1 small onion, minced. Handful of sliced coriander leaves.

For filling......10 almonds blanched and sliced. 50 grams ground paneer or cottage cheese. A few mint leaves, sliced. Salt to taste.

Heat 1 tblsp. oil or ghee and fry onion, ginger, garlic and chillies till soft. Put in kheema, salt, coconut, gram flour and coriander leaves and garam masala and cook till dry and thick. Remove from fire and cool then knead to a smooth mixture. Divide the kheema and filling ingredients into equal number of portions. Form the kheema into cups, stuff with filling, gather the edges together and form into round cutlets. Roll lightly in crumbs and shallow fry till golden brown colour. Drain and serve with chutney of choice.

Shammi kababs (Hyderabad)

500 grams minced meat. 75 grams channa dal. 1-inch piece ginger. 4 flakes garlic. 2 tsps. each of coriander powder and garam masala. Salt and chilli powder to taste. 1 raw egg.

For filling......1 egg, hard-boiled and shelled. 1 medium onion, sliced finely. 8 blanched and sliced almonds. Handful of sliced coriander leaves.

Mix together all the filling ingredients after chopping the egg coarsely. Boil together in salted water both meat and dal till tender and dry. Add ginger, garlic and spices and grind to a very smooth paste. Break in the raw egg and mix well. Divide the meat and the filling ingredients into equal number of portions. Form the meat into a cup, stuff with filling, cover the edges and form into round cutlets. Shallow fry to a golden brown colour. Serve garnished with thinly sliced onion, lime wedges and mint chutney.

Sheekh kababs (Hyderabad)

500 grams minced mutton or kheema. 1 tblsp. each of gram flour and cream. 1-inch piece ginger, minced. 4 flakes

garlic, minced. ½ small bunch of finely sliced coriander leaves. A couple of sliced mint leaves. 4 green chillies, minced. 1 tblsp. garam masala. 1 tsp. each of roasted and ground cumin and coriander seeds. Salt and chilli powder to taste.

Mix all the above ingredients together and set aside for 1 hour. Divide the mutton mixture into lemon-sized balls. Heat and grease the skewers and shape the balls into long cigarettes around the skewers. Grill over charcoal fire or in a hot oven basting occasionally with ghee till cooked and golden brown in colour. Remove carefully from skewers and serve with lime wedges, thin rings of onions and mint chutney.

Palporiyal

500 grams mutton, cut into serving portions. 115 grams sliced onions. 2 cups coconut milk. 1 tblsp. chilli powder. 1 tsp. ground anise seeds. ½ tsp. turmeric powder. Handful of sliced coriander leaves. 2-inch piece minced ginger. Salt to taste.

Heat 5 tblsps. ghee and fry onion and ginger till soft. Put in the turmeric and chilli powder and fry briefly. Add mutton and fry it to a nice red colour. Put in milk of coconut, salt and coriander leaves and cover tightly. Cook over a slow fire till the mutton is tender and completely dry. Sprinkle anise seed powder on top and serve immediately.

Curry puffs

250 grams maida or refined flour. 2 tblsps. melted ghee. Salt to taste.

For filling......250 grams minced mutton or kheema. 2 big onions, finely sliced. 1 tblsp. garam masala. 1 tsp. ground cumin seeds. 1 tsp. cornflour. 2-inch piece ginger, finely sliced. 2 flakes minced garlic. 1 tblsp. grated coconut. Handful of sliced coriander leaves. A big pinch turmeric powder. 1 tsp. coriander powder. Salt to suit the taste.

Mix together flour and salt. Rub in ghee and put in enough cold water to form a stiff dough. Heat 3 tblsps. ghee and put in onion, ginger and garlic and fry till soft. Add ground spices and salt and chilli powder and fry briefly. Put in the rest of the filling ingredients with the exception of cornflour. Cover tightly and cook till the mutton is tender and completely dry without adding any water. Now mix cornflour to a smooth paste with 2 tblsps. water and mix in. Cook till the mixture turns thick. Remove from fire and cool. Roll out the dough as thinly as you can with the help of a little dry flour. Cut into rounds with a biscuit cutter or an inverted glass. Place the mince over one half and fold over to form crescents. Seal and crimp the edges. Deep fry till crisp and golden. Serve hot with chutney of your choice.

Mutton and dal curry

500 grams mutton, cut into serving portions. 125 grams masoor dal. 1 tblsp. coriander powder. 1 tsp. each of ground cumin seeds and garam masala. $\frac{1}{2}$ tsp. turmeric powder. 2 big onions, finely sliced. 4 flakes garlic. 2-inch piece ginger. Salt and chilli powder to taste.

Grind ginger and garlic to a paste and apply on mutton. Cook the dal in water till soft, then pass through a fine sieve. Heat 4 tblsps. ghee and fry the onions till soft. Add all the spices with the exception of garam masala and fry briefly. Add mutton and fry to a nice red colour. Cover with hot water and add salt then cook till the mutton is almost done. Put in the dal, mix well and continue cooking till the mutton is tender. Serve sprinkled with garam masala and coriander leaves.

Mutton molee

500 grams mutton, cut into serving portions. 1 big onion, finely sliced. 4 flakes garlic, minced. 1-inch piece ginger, minced. 1 tsp. each of mustard and fenugreek seeds and turmeric powder. 4 red chillies, chopped. 3 cups thick coconut milk. Salt to taste.

Pound together all the spices. Heat 4 tblsps. ghee and fry onion, ginger and garlic till soft Add ground spices and salt and fry till the onions turn almond coloured. Add mutton and fry to a red colour on all the sides. Pour in coconut milk. Cover tightly and cook till the mutton is tender. Serve hot garnished with coriander leaves.

Kheema

500 grams minced mutton or kheema. 1 cup finely grated coconut. 2 large onions. 4 green chillies, minced. 1 tsp. ground cumin seeds. $\frac{1}{2}$ tsp. mustard seeds. A few curry leaves. 5 red chillies. 2 tblsps. coriander seeds. Salt to taste. $\frac{1}{2}$ tsp. turmeric powder.

Fry onions, red chillies and coriander seeds in a little oil till red and then grind to a smooth paste. Add this paste to the mutton, salt and turmeric powder and enough hot water to cover the mutton and cook till tender and dry. Remove from fire and set aside. Heat 4 tblsps. ghee and put in mustard seeds and curry leaves, when the seeds stop crackling, put in the kheema with the rest of the above ingredients and fry till nicely browned. Serve garnished with coriander leaves.

Mutton curry

500 grams mutton, cut into serving portions. 1 lime-sized ball of tamarind. 1 big onion, sliced finely. 2 medium potatoes, peeled and cubed. 100 grams shelled peas. 5 red chillies. 1 tsp. cumin seeds. $\frac{1}{2}$ tsp. turmeric powder. 1 tblsp. coriander seeds. 5 flakes garlic. 6 peppercorns. 1 tblsp. poppy seeds. $\frac{1}{4}$ tsp. mustard seeds. 1 cardamom. 2 cloves. $\frac{1}{2}$-inch piece cinnamon stick. $\frac{1}{4}$ coconut, finely grated. Handful of sliced coriander leaves. Salt to taste.

Roast together over a dry girdle chillies, garlic, cardamom, cinnamon, cloves, coconut, mustard, cumin, coriander and poppy seeds and grind to a smooth paste. Cover tamarind with water for 5 minutes, then squeeze out the juice or pulp. Heat 4 tblsps. ghee and fry the onions till almond coloured. Add ground paste, turmeric, salt and mutton and fry it to a nice golden colour. Cover with hot water and cook till the mutton is almost done. Put in peas, potatoes and tamarind juice and continue cooking till both the vegetables and the mutton are done. Serve garnished with sliced coriander leaves.

Mutton vindaloo

500 grams mutton, cut into serving portions. 1 lime-sized ball of tamarind. 12 baby potatoes. 12 baby onions. 2 carrots. 1 large tomato, peeled and diced. 50 grams shelled peas. 1 tsp. turmeric powder. 6 red chillies. 6 flakes garlic. 1 tblsp. cumin seeds. 1 big onion, finely sliced. 1-inch piece ginger. 1 tblsp. coriander seeds. $\frac{1}{4}$ tsp. mustard seeds. Salt to taste.

Grind to a paste onion, garlic, chillies, ginger and all the spices. Apply on mutton and set aside for 1 hour. Cover tamarind with water for 5 minutes then squeeze out its juice. Heat 4 tblsps. ghee and fry the mutton to a red colour. Cover with hot water, add salt and tomato and cook till the mutton is almost done. Put in the vegetables and tamarind water and continue cooking till both the the mutton and the vegetables are done. Serve hot.

Mutton and onion mix

500 grams mutton, cut into serving portions. 250 grams baby onions, peeled. 4 flakes garlic. 1-inch piece ginger. 6 green chillies. 1 tbsp. vinegar. 1 tblsp. coriander seeds. 1 tsp. cumin seeds. 8 red chillies. 1 tsp. turmeric powder. 1 large onion, finely sliced. A few curry leaves. Salt to taste. 3 cups thin and 1 cup thick coconut milk. Handful of sliced coriander leaves.

Grind to a paste red chillies, garlic, ginger, green chillies, cumin and coriander seeds. Heat 5 tblsps. ghee and put in sliced onion and curry leaves and fry to a red colour. Add ground paste, turmeric and salt and fry till the ghee floats to the top. Add mutton and fry till brown. Pour in salt and thin coconut milk and cook till the mutton is almost done. Put in the onions and vinegar and continue cooking till both the mutton and the onions are done.

Pour in thick coconut milk and cook till the gravy turns very thick. Serve garnished with coriander leaves.

Mutton kofta curry no. 1

500 grams boiled minced meat or kheema. 2 tblsps. roasted poppy seeds. 1 big onion, minced. 1 tblsp. roasted gram flour. 1 egg. A few curry leaves. 4 green chillies, minced. Salt to taste.

250 grams tomatoes, peeled and diced. 2 cups coconut milk. 25 grams fried and diced cashewnuts. $\frac{1}{2}$ tsp. mustard seeds. 1 tsp. channa dal. 1-inch piece ginger, minced. 4 flakes garlic, minced. $\frac{1}{2}$ tsp. turmeric powder. Handful of coriander leaves. Salt and chilli powder to taste.

Heat 1 tblsp. ghee and fry onion, curry leaves and chillies till soft. Mix with kheema along with poppy seeds and grind to a very smooth paste. Put in gram flour, salt and break in raw egg and knead to a smooth mixture. Form into round balls and deep fry to a golden brown colour. Drain and set aside. Heat 2 tblsp. ghee and put in the mustard seeds and dal. When the dal turns red, put in ginger, garlic and all the spices and fry till soft. Add tomatoes and salt. When the tomatoes turn dry and ghee floats to the top, mix in coconut milk and bring slowly to a boil, reduce heat to simmering and put in the fried koftas. Simmer gently for 5 minutes. Serve hot garnished with cashewnuts and coriander leaves.

Mutton kofta curry no. 2

2 large onions. 1-inch piece ginger. 4 flakes garlic. tblsp. coriander seeds. 2 cloves. $\frac{1}{2}$-inch piece cinnamon stick. 4 cardamoms. 1 tsp. cumin seeds. 2 tblsps. poppy seeds. 4 green chillies, minced. Handful of coriander leaves. 1 tsp. turmeric powder. 2 large tomatoes, peeled and sliced. 4 tblsps. grated coconut. 1 cup thick and 2 cups thin coconut milk. Salt and chilli powder to taste.

For koftas......500 grams boiled minced meat or kheema. 1 small onion. 4 green chillies. 1 tsp. garam masala. 1-inch piece ginger. Handful of coriander leaves. 1 raw egg. Salt to taste.

Grind onion, ginger, garlic, poppy seeds and all the spices to a smooth paste. Grind all the kofta ingredients to a paste. Break in the egg and knead to a smooth mixture. Form into round balls and deep fry to a golden brown colour. Drain and set aside. Heat tblsps. ghee and fry the ground onion mixture till the ghee oozes out. Add tomatoes, salt and turmeric powder and cook till they turn soft and dry. Put in thick coconut milk. Bring to a boil reduce heat to simmering and put in the koftas. Simmer for 5 minutes, put in the thick coconut milk, bring to a boil and remove from fire. Serve garnished with grated coconut and coriander leaves.

Liver curry

500 grams liver, washed and cubed. 1 medium onion, minced. 2 flakes garlic, minced. 1 tblsp. tamarind pulp. 1 tblsp. grated coconut. 1 tblsp. coriander powder. 1 tsp. ground cumin seeds. ¼ tsp. ground mustard seeds. Salt and chilli powder to taste.

Heat 2 tblsps. oil and fry onion and garlic till soft. Add all the spices, mix well then add the liver and 2 tblsps. water cover tightly and cook over a slow fire till the liver is done. Mix in coconut and tamarind juice and cook till dry, then fry till brown and oil oozes out. Serve garnished with coriander leaves.

Liver and potato curry (Mangalore)

500 grams liver, washed and cubed. Lime-sized ball of tamarind. 2 medium potatoes, boiled, peeled and sliced and fried lightly. 2 medium onions. 2 cloves. ½-inch piece cinnamon stick. ¼ coconut. 6 flakes garlic. 1 tsp. cumin seeds. 1 tblsp. coriander powder. ¼ tsp. mustard seeds. ¼ tsp. anise seeds. Salt and chilli powder to taste.

Cover tamarind with water and squeeze out the juice or pulp. Grind onion, coconut, garlic and all the spices to a paste. Boil liver in salt water till tender and dry. Heat 2 tblsps. ghee and fry the ground paste till the ghee floats to the top. Add liver and potatoes, then pour in

the tamarind juice. Cook over a slow fire till the gravy
turns a little thick. Serve hot garnished with sliced coriander leaves.

Liver masala fry (Kerala)

500 grams liver washed and cut into 1-inch cubes. 1 tsp.
coriander seeds. 4 red chillies. 2 cardamoms. 1-inch piece
cinnamon stick. ½ cup finely grated coconut. 1-inch piece
ginger. 1 tblsp. lime juice. 4 cloves. 4 flakes garlic. 1 tsp.
cumin seeds. ½ tsp. turmeric powder. A few curry leaves.
1 tsp. each of mustard and anise seeds. 1 big onion. Salt
to taste.

Powder together cinnamon, cardamoms, cloves and anise
seeds and set aside. Grind together coriander, coconut,
chillies, ginger and garlic to a paste. Mix coconut paste
with liver, add 1 cup water and cook till the liver be-
comes tender and dry. Heat 2 tblsps. oil and put in mustard seeds, when they stop popping, put in sliced onion
and curry leaves and fry onion till it turns light golden
colour. Put in liver and fry to a nice golden colour.
Sprinkle over top ground spices and lime juice before
serving.

Mutton mulotoony

500 grams mutton, cut into serving portions. 2 medium
onions, minced. 4 flakes garlic, sliced. 1-inch piece ginger, minced. 1 tsp. garam masala. 2 medium tomatoes,
peeled and diced. A few curry leaves. 4 red chillies without seeds. 1 tsp. each of ground cumin seeds and coriander powder. ½ tsp. powdered anise seeds. 1 tsp. channa
dal. 1 cup thick coconut milk. ½ tsp. each of pepper and
turmeric powder. 1 lime, cut into thin rings. Salt to taste.

Boil mutton in salted water till tender, drain out the
stock and keep aside. Roast the dal and grind to a paste.
Heat 2 tblsps. ghee and fry onion, ginger and garlic lightly. Put in seasonings and fry briefly. Add tomatoes and
curry leaves. Mix well and then put in the mutton stock.
When the tomatoes turn tender, put in the mutton and

coconut milk after blending it with dal paste and simmer over a gentle fire till the curry turns a little thick. Serve the curry in individual plates garnished with lime rings.

Chicken Mulotoony

1 chicken, disjointed. 1 tblsp. ground coriander seeds. ¼ tsp. ground mustard seeds. ½ tsp. each of ground cumin and poppy seeds. ½ tsp. turmeric powder. 5 red chillies. 1-inch piece ginger. 4 flakes garlic. 1 big piece coconut. 1 lime-sized ball of tamarind. 1 big onion, sliced finely. A few curry leaves. Salt to taste.

Soak tamarind in 4 cups water for 5 minutes then squeeze out the pulp. Grind together chillies, ginger, garlic and coconut and mix into the tamarind along with all the spices and salt. Put chicken in a vessel, cover with tamarind water and cook till the chicken turns tender. Remove from fire and set aside. Heat 3 tblsps. ghee and put in onion and curry leaves, when the onion turns brown pour over the chicken and serve hot.

Chilli fry

250 grams boneless mutton, cubed. 1 big onion, finely sliced. 6 green chillies, slitted. 4 red chillies, broken into bits. ½ cup tamarind water. ½ tsp turmeric powder. Salt to taste.

Put all the above ingredients in a vessel and cover tightly. Cook without adding water till the mutton is tender and dry. Put in 3 tblsps. oil and fry the mutton to a nice brown colour. Serve hot.

Chicken curry (Hyderabad)

1 chicken, disjointed. ½ coconut, finely grated. 1 medium onion, minced. 4 flakes garlic, minced. ½-inch piece ginger, minced. 250 grams tomatoes, blanched and sliced. 2 cardamoms. 4 cloves. 1-inch piece cinnamon stick. ¾ tsp. turmeric powder. 1 tsp. ground cumin seeds. A big pinch

each of mace and nutmeg. Salt and lime juice to taste.
Handful of sliced coriander leaves.

Powder together all the whole spices. Heat 5 tblsps. ghee
and fry onion, ginger and garlic till soft. Add all the
spices and salt and fry briefly. Put in the chicken and
fry to a red colour. Add coconut and tomatoes. Cover
tightly till the tomatoes turn soft and dry. Pour in 2
cups hot water, continue cooking till the chicken is done.
Serve hot sprinkled with lime juice and coriander leaves.

Baked chicken (Hyderabad)

1 whole chicken, cleaned. 2 small onions. 1-inch piece
ginger. 4 red chillies. 1 tsp. each of garam masala and
ground cumin seeds. 3 flakes garlic. 1 cup beaten curds.
A few drops orange red food colouring.

Cut deep slits all over the body of the chicken with the
help of a sharp knife. Grind onion, ginger, garlic and
chillies to a paste and mix into the curds along with all
the remaining spices and 2 tblsps. ghee. Rub the mixture
thoroughly on the chicken and set aside for a few hours.
Bake the chicken in preheated (375°F) oven till done
or grill on a charcoal fire after fixing it in skewers.

Chicken treat

1 chicken, disjointed. 1 coconut. 125 grams rice. 2 cups
thick coconut milk. 2 big onions. 6 red chillies. ½ tsp.
turmeric powder. 2 tsps. coriander seeds. 12 peppercorns.
½ tsp. mustard seeds. 3 cloves. 1 tsp. poppy seeds. 1 tsp.
cumin seeds. 1 lime-sized ball of tamarind. ½-inch piece
cinnamon stick. 4 flakes garlic. Salt to suit the taste.

Steam-cook the chicken after applying salt to it. Fry
half the coconut, onions, garlic, chillies and all the spices
in oil till a nice brown colour and grind to a paste. Cover
tamarind in water for 5 minutes, then squeeze out the
pulp. Soak rice in water for 1 hour, drain and grind to a
paste with salt and remaining half coconut. Place the
mixture on a slow fire and cook till thick. Remove from

fire, cool and knead to a smooth mixture, form into small flat and round cakes and steam till cooked. In a vessel pour 4 tblsps. oil and then put in the ground onion paste and chicken pieces and fry till the chicken turns brown. Pour in coconut milk and tamarind water and bring slowly to a boil, reduce heat to simmering and put in the rice cakes. Cook till the gravy turns thick. Serve piping hot.

Malayalam chicken curry

1 medium chicken. 25 large padvals. 2 medium onions. 2-inch piece ginger. 6 flakes garlic. 6 green chillies. 4 cloves. 4 cardamoms. 2-inch piece cinnamon stick. 1 tsp. turmeric powder. 4 red chillies. 1 tsp. cumin seed.s 3 cups coconut milk. Salt and chilli powder to taste.

Grind onion, ginger, garlic, chillies and all the spices to a paste. Steam-cook the chicken. Remove flesh from its bones and grind to a paste. Mix in half the ground spice paste and set aside. Wash the padvals. Make a cut lengthwise in each padval and remove the seeds and pulp from inside. Heat 2 tblsps. oil and fry the chicken mixture to a light brown colour. Cool and stuff the padvals through the slits. Heat 3 tblsps. oil in a pan and put in the remaining spice paste and fry to a golden colour. Add the padvals and fry them gently till lightly browned. Pour in the coconut milk and cook over a slow fire till the padvals turn tender and gravy thick. Serve garnished with sliced corriander leaves.

Pork Vindaloo (Mangalore)

1 kilo pork. 8 red chillies. 2 green chillies. 1-inch piece ginger. 4 flakes garlic. 1 tsp. turmeric powder. 1 tsp. cumin seeds. 6 peppercorns. 2 medium onions. 1 lime-sized ball of tamarind. 2 tblsps. vinegar. 1 tsp. sugar. Salt to suit the taste.

Cut the pork into pieces and cover with boiling water. Add salt and cook till tender and dry, then put in 4 tblsps. oil and fry till brown. Remove from fire and keep aside. Cover tamarind with water for 5 minutes, then squeeze out the pulp. Grind together onion, ginger, garlic, chillies and all the spices to a paste. Heat 4 tblsps. oil and fry the ground paste to a golden brown colour. Add vinegar, tamarind juice, salt and sugar, stir till the sugar dissolves then put in the pork. Cook till the gravy turns quite thick. Remove and serve hot.

Pork Indad (Mangalore)

1 kilo pork, cut into serving portions. 10 red chillies. 1 medium onion. 1 tsp. turmeric powder. 1 lime-sized ball of tamarind. 6 flakes garlic. 8 peppercorns. 5 cloves. $\frac{1}{2}$-inch piece cinnamon stick. 2 tblsps. vinegar. 1 tblsp. sugar. 3 tblsps. brandy. 150 grams boiled baby potatoes. Salt to taste.

Grind to a paste chillies, onion, tamarind, garlic and all the whole spices. Heat 4 tblsps. oil and fry the ground paste till the oil floats to the top. Put in the pork and fry to a golden brown colour. Add the remaining ingredients with the exception of potatoes. Mix well and cover with boiling water. Cook till the pork is almost done, then put in the potatoes and continue cooking till the pork turns tender. Remove and serve hot.

Coorgi Pork Vindaloo

1 kilo pork, cut into serving portions. 20 red chillies. 6 medium onions. 1 tblsp. cumin seeds. 1 tsp. turmeric powder. 1 tblsp. corriander powder. 8 peppercorns. 2 tblsps. vinegar. 2 medium potatoes, boiled and sliced and fried lightly. Salt to taste.

Grind together onions, chillies and all the spices to a paste. Mix into the pork and put in a vessel. Add salt and cover with boiling water, cover and cook till the pork is almost done. Add vinegar and potatoes and continue cooking till the pork is tender and gravy thick. Serve hot.

FISH AND EGGS

6 eggs, hard-boiled. 1 big onion, minced. 1 flake garlic, minced. ½-inch piece ginger, minced. 1 tsp. each of ground corriander seeds and cumin seeds. ½ tsp. turmeric powder. 4 green chillies, slitted. 2 cups coconut milk. 1 medium tomato, peeled and sliced. Handful of sliced corriander leaves. Salt and chilli powder to taste.

Shell and cut eggs into halves lengthwise. Heat 2 tblsps. oil and fry ginger, garlic and onion till soft. Add all the spices and fry briefly. Put in the tomato and salt and cook till the oils starts separating out. Pour in the coconut milk, add green chillies and bring slowly to a boil, reduce heat and put in the eggs. Simmer gently till the gravy turns a little thick. Serve hot garnished with corriander leaves.

Egg molee

4 hard-boiled eggs shelled and cut into halves lengthwise. 50 grams boiled green peas. 2 cups coconut juice. 1 tsp. ground cumin seeds. ½ tsp. turmeric powder. 1 small onion, minced. 2 green chillies, minced. ½-inch piece ginger, minced. Handful of sliced corriander leaves. 1 medium tomato, blanched and sliced. Salt and chilli powder to taste. ½ tsp. garam masala.

Heat 2 tblsps. oil and fry onion and ginger and chillies till soft. Add all the spices and fry briefly. Put in the tomatoes, peas and salt. Cook till the tomatoes turn soft and the oil oozes out. Add coconut milk and bring slowly to a boil, reduce heat to simmering and put in the eggs. Continue cooking till the gravy turns thick. Serve garnished with corriander leaves.

Omellete

2 eggs, separated. 1 tblsp. each of cream and milk. (Optional). 4 green chillies, minced. 1 small onion,

minced. Handful of sliced corriander leaves. A few sliced mint leaves. ½-inch piece ginger, minced. 1 tiny tomato, minced. Salt to taste.

Beat egg whites till frothy. Beat yolks with salt until thick and fold into whites along with the rest of the above ingredients. Grease a pan liberally with ghee and pour the mixture into it, spread it evenly and cook over a slow fire till the bottom turns a delicate brown, then turn over. When both the sides turn light brown, put a teaspoon of butter on one end of the omellete and roll like a jelly roll. Remove and serve piping hot with fried potatoes and ketchup.

Egg curry (Mangalore)

4 hard-boiled eggs, shelled and cut into halves lengthwise. 2 small onions, minced. 1 lime-sized ball of tamarind. 1 tsp. ground cumin seeds. A big pinch of pepper. 1 medium potato, boiled, peeled and cubed and fried lightly. ½ tsp. turmeric powder. Salt to taste.

Heat 2 tblsps. oil and fry the onions till soft. Add all the spices and fry briefly. Add 1 cup tamarind water. (To make tamarind water, put tamarind in water for 5 minutes and squeeze out the water) bring slowly to a boil, reduce heat to simmering and put in the eggs and potatoes and simmer till the gravy turns a little thick. Remove from fire and serve hot.

Egg indad (Mangalore)

4 hard-boiled eggs, shelled and cut into halves lengthwise. 2 medium potatoes, boiled, peeled, cubed and fried lightly. 4 red chillies. ½ tsp. cumin seeds. ½ tsp. turmeric powder. 2 green chillies. 1 medium onion. ½-inch piece ginger. 2 flakes garlic. 1 tsp. each of vinegar and sugar. 2 big tomatoes, blanched and sliced. Salt to suit the taste. Handful of sliced corriander leaves.

Grind onion, ginger and garlic and all the spices to a paste in vinegar. Heat 2 tblsps. ghee and fry the ground masala nicely. Put in sugar, salt and tomatoes and cook till the tomatoes turn soft. Pour in 1 cup water, bring slowly to a boil, reduce heat to simmering and put in the eggs. Simmer till the gravy turns a little thick. Serve garnished with corriander leaves.

Roasted fish

1 whole fish. 1 tsp. turmeric powder. 1 tblsp. cumin seeds. 6 flakes garlic. 1-inch piece ginger. 6 red chillies. 1 lime-sized ball of tamarind.

Clean, scale and gut the fish. Remove fishy smell (see helpful hints) then make gashes on both the sides of the fish with the help of a sharp knife. Cover tamarind with water for 5 minutes, then squeeze out the pulp. Grind the rest of the ingredients to a paste and mix in the tamarind juice. Rub the paste well on the fish and roast on an open fire basting occasionally with oil till tender and golden coloured. Serve it on a bed of sliced rings of onions, cucumbers and tomatoes. And garnish the whole with fried cashewnuts and wedges of lime.

Mean Pinpudu

1 medium fish. 5 red chillies. 1-inch piece ginger, sliced. 4 green chillies, minced. 1 medium onion, minced. ¼ tsp. turmeric powder. 1 tsp. cumin seeds. 4 flakes garlic. 2 tblsps. thick tamarind juice. ½ coconut. Salt to taste.

Clean, scale and gut the fish. Remove fishy smell . . . . see helpful hints. Grind and extract thick milk from coconut. Cut the fish halfway through lengthwise and remove the centre bone. Heat 2 tblsps. ghee and put in ginger, chillies, onion and garlic and fry till soft. Add tamarind and powdered red chillies, salt and all the spices and fry till thick. Remove from fire and stuff this mixture into the fish. Also rub some of it on the body of the fish. Heat a tblsp. of ghee in a pan and place a plantain leaf over it. Grease it with ghee and place the fish over it. Pour the coconut milk on it and cover the fish nicely with another plantain leaf. Cover tightly and cook over a slow fire till the fish is done. Serve hot.

Fish curry

500 grams fish. A few curry leaves. $\frac{1}{4}$ coconut. 1 lime-sized ball of tamarind. 1 medium onion. 4 green chillies. 1 small bunch corriander leaves. $\frac{1}{2}$ tsp. mustard seeds. $\frac{1}{2}$ tsp. turmeric powder. 1 tsp. ground cumin seeds. Salt and chilli powder to taste.

Soak tamarind in 2 cups water for 5 minutes, then extract the juice. Grind onion, coconut, chillies and corriander leaves. Wash and cut the fish into slices, then remove fishy smell (see helpful hints). Heat 4 tblsps. oil and put in the mustard seeds and curry leaves. When the mustard seeds stop popping, put in the coconut paste and fry nicely, add the fish and mix nicely into the masala. Put in the tamarind water, the remaining spices and salt. Cover tightly and cook till the fish is done. Serve with boiled rice.

Meen Molee

500 grams fish. 2 cups thick coconut milk. $\frac{1}{2}$ tsp. turmeric powder. 1 medium onion, minced. 1-inch piece ginger, minced. 4 flakes garlic, minced. 6 green chillies, slitted. 1 big tomato, sliced. 1 tsp. ground cumin seeds. 8 cashew-nuts. Salt to taste.

Clean and cut the fish into slices. Remove fishy smell (see helpful hints). Heat 2 tblsps. ghee and fry onion, ginger and garlic till soft. Add all the spices, salt and tomato and cook till the tomato turns dry. Put in the fish, chillies and cashewnuts. Mix well then pour in the coconut milk. Cover tightly and cook till the fish is done. Serve hot.

Prawn vindaloo

500 grams prawns. 6 flakes garlic. $\frac{1}{2}$ tsp. each of cumin and mustard seeds. 1 tsp. turmeric powder. 1-inch piece ginger. 5 red chillies. 1 lime-sized ball of tamarind. 1 tblsp. vinegar. 3 medium onions, minced. Salt to taste. 1 tsp. garam masala.

Grind tamarind, ginger, garlic, chillies, mustard and cumin seeds to a paste. Shell and clean and devein the prawns. Apply on them salt and turmeric powder and set aside for half an hour. Heat 4 tblsps. oil and fry the onions to a golden colour. Add ground masala paste along with all the spices and salt and fry it nicely. Put in prawns and vinegar. Mix well, then pour in 1 cup water. Cover and cook till the prawns are tender and dry.

Masala prawns

500 grams prawns. 500 grams onions, minced. 1 tblsp. cumin seeds. 1 tsp. turmeric powder. 8 red chillies. 2 tblsps. vinegar. 8 flakes garlic. $\frac{1}{2}$ coconut. A few curry leaves. Salt to taste.

Clean, devein and wash the prawns. Grind all the above ingredients to a paste and apply on prawns and set aside for half an hour or so. Heat 4 tblsps. oil and fry the onions till limp. Put in the prawns and cover tightly. Cook over a slow fire without adding any water till the prawns are tender, then fry till red. Serve garnished with corriander leaves.

Prawn and brinjal curry

500 grams prawns, shelled and deveined. 1 large brinjal, sliced. 1 tblsp. corriander seeds. 1 tblsp. cumin seeds. 1 tsp. turmeric powder. 2 tblsp. finely sliced coconut. 2 big tomatoes, blanched and sliced. 2 cups thick coconut milk. 1 big onion, minced. 4 flakes garlic, minced. Salt and lemon juice to suit the taste. Handful of sliced corriander leaves.

Fry sliced coconut to a red colour. Powder all the spices. Apply salt and turmeric on prawns and set aside for half an hour. Heat 4 tblsps. oil and put in onion and garlic, then add all the spices and fry briefly, put in tomatoes and cook till soft. Add prawns and cook till the mixture turns dry. Mix in the brinjals and pour in the coconut milk. Cover and cook till the prawns and brinjals are cooked. Serve garnished with fried coconut and corriander leaves and sprinkle lime juice on the whole.

Prawn curry

500 grams prawns, shelled and deveined. 125 grams tomatoes, peeled and sliced. 2 cups coconut milk. 1 medium onion, minced. 4 flakes garlic, minced. ½ tsp. turmeric powder. A few curry leaves. 4 green chillies, slitted. 4 red chillies. Handful of corriander leaves. 1 tblsp. each of cumin and corriander seeds. 1-inch piece ginger, minced. Salt to taste.

Powder together all the spices and red chillies. Apply salt and turmeric on prawns and set aside for half an hour, or so. Heat 4 tblsps. ghee and add onion, ginger and garlic and salt and fry till soft. Add prawns and fry till dry. Add curry leaves and tomatoes. When the mixture turns dry, add green chillies and pour in coconut milk. Cook till the prawns are tender. Serve garnished with corriander leaves.

Hot and spicy prawns (Kerala)

40 large prawns. 1 lime-sized ball of tamarind. A few curry leaves. 20 red chillies. 1 tsp. fenugreek seeds. 2 tblsps. corriander seeds. 12 flakes garlic. 1 tblsp. turmeric powder. 10 green chillies. 1-inch piece ginger. 250 grams finely sliced onions. Salt to suit the taste. 1 tsp. mustard seeds.

Roast together fenugreek, mustard and corriander seeds and pound finely. Shell and wash the prawns nicely. Apply salt and turmeric and set aside for half an hour. Grind together chillies, ginger, garlic and onions coarsely. Cover tamarind with 2 cups water for 5 minutes, then squeeze out the juice. Heat 5 tblsps. oil and fry the curry leaves and ground onion paste lightly, mix in the prawns and ground spices and tamarind water and cook till the prawns are completely dry and tender. Serve garnished with corriander leaves.

Dry masala prawns

Shell and devein prawns and mix with salt, turmeric and chilli powder. String and put them out in the hot sun for

5 to 10 days to dry completely. Store in airtight containers. When wanted for use fry the prawns in oil till crisp. Drain, cool and pound to a fine powder along with cumin seeds and some garam masala. Serve on rice or on vegetable curries. You can also prepare the shells of prawns in the same way. Wash the shells nicely and then deep fry till crisp and golden. Drain, cool and powder and then eat and see how you enjoy your meals.

Konchu Theeyal (Kerala)

500 grams prawns, cleaned, shelled and deveined. 1 drumstick, scraped and diced into small pieces. ½ coconut. 2 medium onions. 1 tblsp. corriander seeds. 8 red chillies. ½ tsp. fenugreek seeds. A few curry leaves. 1 lime-sized ball of tamarind. Salt to taste.

Cover tamarind with 1 cup hot water for 5 minutes and then squeeze out the pulp. Fry the rest of the ingredients with the exception of prawns in a little oil to a nice golden colour and grind to a paste. Mix into the tamarind. Heat the tamarind and add the prawns and drumsticks and cook till both are done. Serve hot.